OUR DAY
AND

THE WORDS OF

GENERATION

EDWARD M. KENNEDY

Edited by HENRY STEELE COMMAGER

With a Foreword by ARCHIBALD MACLEISH

SIMON AND SCHUSTER · NEW YORK

PUBLISHED BY SIMON AND SCHUSTER
A DIVISION OF GULF & WESTERN CORPORATION
SIMON & SCHUSTER BUILDING
ROCKEFELLER CENTER
1230 AVENUE OF THE AMERICAS
NEW YORK, NEW YORK 10020

DESIGNED BY EVE METZ
PHOTO EDITOR: VINCENT VIRGA
MANUFACTURED IN THE UNITED STATES OF AMERICA
PRINTED AND BOUND BY THE MURRAY PTG. CO., FORGE VILLAGE, MASS.

1   2   3   4   5   6   7   8   9   10

LIBRARY OF CONGRESS CATALOGING IN PUBLICATION DATA

KENNEDY, EDWARD MOORE, 1932–
    OUR DAY AND GENERATION.

    1. UNITED STATES—POLITICS AND GOVERNMENT—1945–
—ADDRESSES, ESSAYS, LECTURES.   2. UNITED STATES—
ECONOMIC POLICY—1971–   —ADDRESSES, ESSAYS, LECTURES.
3. UNITED STATES—SOCIAL POLICY—ADDRESSES, ESSAYS,
LECTURES.   4. UNITED STATES—FOREIGN RELATIONS—1945–
—ADDRESSES, ESSAYS, LECTURES.   I. COMMAGER, HENRY
STEELE, 1902–   II. TITLE.
E838.5.K382   1979   309.1'73'092   79-17550
ISBN 0-671-24133-8

CONTENTS

To
ROSE FITZGERALD KENNEDY

ROSE is the finest teacher we ever had. She made our home a university that surpassed any formal classroom in the exciting quest for knowledge. With her gentle games and questions, she could bring the farthest reaches of the university to our dinner table, or transform the daily headlines into new and stimulating adventures in understanding.

She could diagram a sentence, bisect an angle in geometry, or conjugate a Latin verb. She could spot a hole in a sock from a hundred yards away. She could catch an error in our grammar, or sense a wandering eye at the grace before our meals. She could recite "The Midnight Ride of Paul Revere," name the capital of any nation in the world, and bring alive the history of every place we went.

She did everything nine times. And now she's doing everything twenty-nine times again. For half a century in ways like these, she has been gently stretching each child and grandchild toward her goal of excellence. And always, she mixed her tonic of education and self-improvement with a dose of love so overflowing that her potion was irresistible.

She was also the quiet at the center of the storm, the anchor of the family, the safe harbor where little ones could tow their capsized boats and set their sails again, confident her hand was on the tiller.

For all of us, sons and daughters, she has been the rock and foundation of our lives, making our family standards both livable and reachable. She has shaped our dreams and goals, supported our public and private causes, encouraged us in our service to others in return for the many blessings we have had.

Her children have been doubly blessed. We have had our father's drive and our mother's grace, our father's love of action and our mother's love of history and scholarship, our father's gift of athletics and our mother's gift of politics.

She is a symbol of the best in us, a constant inspiration that helps us meet the challenge of the future. In so many ways, she is the fulfillment of the ancient wisdom of the poet Pindar, who wrote, "A graceful and honorable old age is the childhood of immortality."

Georgetown University   EDWARD M. KENNEDY
Washington, D.C.
October 1, 1977

PREFACE

FEW SENATORS OF OUR GENERATION have spoken more consistently, more eloquently, or more perspicaciously on major public issues than Edward Kennedy of Massachusetts, who is, rightly, ever conscious that he is a successor to John Quincy Adams and Daniel Webster. Over a stretch of sixteen years now he has addressed himself to every major public issue before the American people, and anticipated some of which they were not as yet aware. Nor has he distinguished between the domestic and foreign areas, for he is one of the few members of Congress who knows that these are inseparable.

This collection of extracts from his public speeches addresses itself inevitably to the great issues which have enlisted the Senator's interests and passions over the past two decades. To the student of politics these concerns recapitulate those of the American people; to the student of history they mirror the people themselves. A consistent philosophy animates these observations and admonitions, a common loyalty dictates them, a public morality inspires them. The philosophy is that of democracy, the loyalty that of devotion to the commonwealth, the morality that of compassion and justice.

The whole of Mr. Kennedy's senatorial career might rightly be read as an extensive commentary on the preamble of our Constitution, for it has been devoted to realizing a more perfect union, justice, domestic tranquility, the common defense, the general welfare, and liberty. Few other senators of our time have committed themselves as consistently to these objectives.

This selection is inevitably and even tantalizingly brief, but it is not inconclusive. A definite intellectual and moral pattern emerges: a pattern of confidence in the democratic processes and in the ability of an informed people to make the decisions which will preserve the Republic in all its authority and integrity.

In one of his most recent speeches, Senator Kennedy asked the question Benjamin Franklin had asked at the close of the convention which drafted our Constitution: "Is it a rising or a setting sun?" This is, in a very real sense, the question to which Senator Kennedy has addressed himself, with almost passionate urgency. It is clear that notwithstanding the dangers that glare upon us and the fears that beset us, Senator Kennedy himself is confident that the nation which in the past triumphed over adversity can "summon the will to meet and conquer any challenge." But this is not enough. It is not, after all, our destiny to be the creature of circumstances, but rather to form and master those circumstances. What Senator Kennedy is saying is pretty much what that other Massachusetts man, Ralph Waldo Emerson, said over a century ago: "Power can be generous," and "the very grandeur of the means which offer themselves to us should suggest grandeur in our own conduct."

In making these selections, I have had the invaluable help of my research assistant, Mary E. Powlesland, who shares my admiration for the role which the Senator has played, and my expectations for the role he is destined to play in the future.

HENRY STEELE COMMAGER

Amherst, Massachusetts
June 1979

FOREWORD

FAMOUS SENATORS and the distinguished historians who write about them do not often meet in a book. One is usually gone before the other gets there. In this book, however, Edward Kennedy and Henry Commager have found each other on the page. They are both men of the century and they recognize each other, for all the difference in their ages. Edward Kennedy at forty-seven is not only the dominant figure in the contemporary Senate but the acknowledged leader of his generation in the country, and Henry Commager, though older, is still what he has been for fifty years, *the* political historian of our time. Which means that when this Senator's published addresses are edited by this historian, as they are here, they find their place not only among the documents of these years but among their events. The Senator's concern with education and with public health and with inflation becomes a part of the sense of crisis which increases with all of us as the decade of the seventies closes and that other, unknown decade opens on beyond.

But, with Edward Kennedy, the concern becomes a part of the apprehension in a different way. He is aware that we live at a moment of crisis such as we have not had to face before, either in the First World War or the Second or the Great Depression which lay between or the hysterical subversion of the McCarthy years which followed. He knows that we live at the beginning or the end (it is hard to say which) of the crisis of the family which produced the crisis of the city with its rotting streets and murderous children, and the crisis of the schools, the drugs, the handguns. But he knows, too, that the country is still strong and that its government can function. He believes in government—in the Senate as an instrument of government, in legislation as the instrument of the Senate. From the beginning of his public life he has believed in government by the Senate. He has become, in brief, that rarest of senators, a senator who is first and foremost a public servant with a public servant's responsibilities.

Friends and newspaper reporters and interested advocates of one cause or another have persistently attempted to involve him in the customary presidential candidacy which diverts and eventually destroys a senatorial career, but Kennedy himself has put first things first, with the result that he is now one of the very few modern American senators who can be ranked—who *must* be ranked—with the most distinguished of their historical predecessors.

And the result is that when he speaks of the problems of the Republic as he does in these papers, he speaks not as a politician engaged in exploiting problems for his own or his party's political advancement but as a public servant dedicated to their solution. No honest man who knows the facts would permit himself to imply by any form of words that the young Senator's interest in public health over the past many years has been merely political. The Senator's words give no countenance to that kind of interpretation. And besides, there are easier ways to become a presidential possibility than to challenge a rich and unforgiving pressure group like the AMA. When he talks about public health he talks not to the galleries but to the truly concerned, and not to possible future voters but to present sufferers from impossible conditions. He speaks, in other words, *for* the problem—for the *solution* of the problem. And the voice is a persuasive voice, a quiet voice:

> People today are not asking much from government. They are asking for the simple things that make a difference . . . They want jobs where they can work . . . They want prices at the supermarket their budgets can afford. They want schools that can bring their children a decent education. They want health care to be a basic right for all, not just an expensive privilege for the few. They want safe streets where they can walk at night . . .

This voice knows what it is talking about when it says, "They want." It knows that they *do* want. There has been a great deal of blather over the last year, beginning in California and blowing east against the sun, about what Americans are *supposed* to want: less government, no government at all. We are disillusioned, the prophets tell us—disillusioned with our government of ourselves.

All one has to do to judge that kind of talk is to read Senator Kennedy's quiet sentences. What the American people want is what they have always wanted—*better* government. And better government, in the legislative branch, means not less government but more creative government—a government which will no longer wait on the White House to propose legislation, or on professional lobbyists to demand it, or on the National Rifle Association to forbid it, but will itself assume the initiative of preparing for the need when the need arises: working out its position for itself, accepting its constitutional responsibilities, and so enacting the legislation which should be enacted, repealing the legislation which should be repealed.

And this, of course, is precisely what Senator Kennedy has been concerned with for years past, as these papers prove. He has been preparing the legislative position, arming the Senate to take considered action in its constitutional sphere both on the domestic and on the foreign front. For the foreign responsibilities of the Senate, as Mr. Kennedy sees them, are not only to advise and consent (or dissent) after policies have been proposed to it by the President, but also to help shape the international presence of the American people by representing their true concerns: their commitment to peace, to the strength and restraint necessary for peace; to human rights and human aspirations; to international control of international dangers like terrorism and the proliferation of nuclear arms. For the last ten years he has been urging the long view of our role in world affairs because it is the view native to our people. They recognize the new and necessary interdependence of nations and are ready to practice it, and Senator Kennedy has become one of its truly representative voices in this changing time.

Which, perhaps, is why these occasional papers of his tell us more about the real state of the American mind—the state of the Union—than the professional news media tell us, to say nothing of the professional pollsters or propagandists. The media proceed, for obvious and understandable reasons, on the assumption that what concerns us as a people is what excites us: the dramatic event, the imminent disaster, the noble intervention in the cause of peace. But the truth is that in real life there are family concerns, private concerns, *under* the excitement, under the drama, which strike far more deeply home—the concerns the Senator speaks of in those honest words: concerns of families which cannot pay their hospital bills; of families whose savings are losing value from week to week and year to year; of families whose high-school children cannot read or write and whose dropout children find no jobs; of families whose lives as families are poisoned by inner-city crime and inner-city drugs and inner-city filth.

These, to multitudes of Americans, are the real realities of their lives, the real realities of life in America. And, to the senior Senator from Massachusetts, what affects life in America will sooner or later affect America itself unless those who are charged with responsiblity for the conduct of government are prepared to act. To act actively and not passively. Imaginatively and not reluctantly.

As I read through these pages, I think of the voice that speaks in these excerpts —these paragraphs—and I wonder how a man as young as Edward Kennedy, born in our Northeast corner, our New England, brought up in a family of comfortable means, has learned to speak as well as he speaks for the whole country, for the multitudes of people who make up our country now. But then I remember that Thomas Jefferson, Theodore Roosevelt and Franklin Roosevelt were all provincial and all born to wealth and that they too spoke for the whole of the American people. It is not, I think, a matter merely of the pronouns—that political "we" the candidates for office use. Kennedy's "we" has a deeper tone of relationship and belonging, and my guess would be that it comes from the profession he has practiced with such single-mindedness so many years— the profession of the public servant. It is the tradition of the old historic Senate that we hear now in this young, cool, eager voice.

ARCHIBALD MacLEISH

Conway, Massachusetts
June 1979

LET US DEVELOP THE RESOURCES OF OUR LAND, CALL
FORTH ITS POWERS, BUILD UP ITS INSTITUTIONS,
PROMOTE ALL ITS GREAT INTERESTS, AND SEE
WHETHER WE ALSO, IN OUR DAY AND GENERATION, MAY NOT
PERFORM SOMETHING WORTHY TO BE REMEMBERED.

—DANIEL WEBSTER,
Address at the laying of the cornerstone
of the Bunker Hill Monument,
Charlestown, Massachusetts, June 17, 1825

THE TIME
HAS COME

With Webster, "I speak not as a Massachusetts man, not as a Northerner. I speak as an American, hear me for my cause."

I do not expect you to agree with my stand on all of these questions. But those who seek only approval will find themselves scorned by persons of conscience and concern. So I speak to you of challenges that we must face together if this nation is to fulfill the vision of its founders.

I want to turn over to my children—as you do—a nation that is no longer at war. I want to turn over to my children—as you do—a nation that is no longer divided against itself by racial hatred, a nation that is no longer blind to the filth of its rivers and lakes, a nation that is no longer unable to find jobs for six million of its citizens. I want to turn over to my children—as you do—a nation that has not grown indifferent to the individuals who live within it.

FEBRUARY 27, 1971

We were discovered as a nation because five hundred years ago an Italian sailor had the courage of his convictions and sailed westward into the unknown. We are called America because another Italian explorer came to these shores and recorded the geography of our coastline. We became the United States of America because two hundred years ago the inhabitants of thirteen separate colonies, all immigrants or children or grandchildren of immigrants, had the courage of their convictions and joined together to resist tyranny and dedicate themselves to freedom and liberty.

OCTOBER 12, 1970

17

America was an idea shaped in the turbulence of revolution, then given formal structure in a constitution. That idea—that set of principles—has been the foundation, the guide, and the destination, for two centuries of American history. We have fought over its meaning, defended it against foreign enemies, struggled to adapt it to new conditions. But we have never abandoned it. Nor can we. For it is what we are. Not a continent, not an arsenal, not wealth and factories—but a democratic republic. Call it democracy or freedom; call it human liberty or individual opportunity, equality or justice. But underneath, they are all the same—the belief in the right and capacity of every individual to govern himself, and to share in governing the necessary institutions of social order.

MAY 14, 1978

Two hundred years ago beacon fires were lighted on New England hilltops as people who loved their freedom spread the news of Lexington and Concord and the beginning of the American Revolution.

We can light those beacon fires again. From the hilltops of America, we can send another sort of call to arms, a call for more effective action on all the challenges that face us.

SEPTEMBER 30, 1978

The dreams and goals of the men and women of Massachusetts have always been an inspiration to others in the nation. We yield to none in the beauty of the sandy shores of Cape Cod, or our lovely mountains and valleys in the Berkshires. We are proud of our role in public and private education, in medicine and health, in science and engineering, in literature and the arts.

JANUARY 24, 1974

I see a new America, an America in the sunlight, an America that is truly free and open, ready to test itself against all the great challenges of our time. I also see a new and stronger people in America, a people proud of their country and jealous of their freedom, a people vigilant against any abuse of government, demanding better answers from their leaders and better vision for the future.

APRIL 13, 1976

We have unlocked the nuclear secret and devised weapons of unbelievably destructive capacity; but can we prevent them from ever being used? We have discovered valuable minerals deep within the earth and under the seas and developed the technologies to use them; but can we conserve them for the use of future generations and ensure that their development aids all the peoples of the world? We have crafted a system of legal and political institutions of enormous complexity; but can we guarantee justice and equity to every American? We have built the world's most productive economic system; but can we end the distortions that imperil economic growth and that deny the fruits of that progress to millions of people? We have achieved miraculous advances in medical science, transplanting vital organs from one human being to another and exploring the mystery of life itself; but can we assure that all our people have access to quality health care? Can we control the advances of science so that mankind is the beneficiary?

JUNE 17, 1976

The melting pot of America has made the whole of our nation greater than the sum of its parts.

OCTOBER 12, 1970

Perhaps never before in the history of the world has there been an emblem so full of the great aspirations of all men everywhere as the flag of the United States. Countless generations of immigrants have sought a new life and new world in America, drawn by the Stars and Stripes and the promise of liberty and freedom.

The flag our forebears received at their citizenship ceremony initiated them into the life of love and freedom, and they went forth to build a new nation. Our common aspirations today are as boundless as the mind of man. They surpass all contemporary debate. They exceed even the deepest divisions of our time, because they reflect the timeless quest of men to be free, to live in a society that is open, where the principles of freedom and justice and equality prevail.

It is for this reason that patriotism and the flag can never be the special preserve of any particular party or any particular political philosophy. I love the flag no less because I believe that America has lost its way in Vietnam. I love the flag no less because I want America to move ahead to right the wrongs we see in our society at home. Those of us who push America on do so out of love and hope for the

America that can be. We are full of the awareness of how much is right with America, how much we have done in years gone by to fulfill the promise of democracy for all our people.

JULY 4, 1970

The temptation to surrender to our present difficulties, to endure them rather than take arms against them, is understandable. But it is not acceptable. It is at odds with America's heritage and character. It is false to the pioneer spirit that built this country and made it great.

JUNE 14, 1979

The time has come to meet the serious challenges we face on issues like housing and education, energy and transportation, crime control, and human rights at home and overseas.

The time has come to adopt a program of national health insurance, so that we can control the cost of health care and bring better care to those who need it most.

The time has come to ratify the Equal Rights and D.C. Voting Rights amendments, and end the unfair discrimination against women in our society and the citizens of the District of Columbia.

The time has come to make a stronger effort to enforce the laws and ensure that no state government, no city council, no sheriff, no school board or university system is above the law.

JANUARY 22, 1979

Now is the time to reduce the monopoly power of massive selfish-interest groups over our economy.

Now is the time to end the excessive burden of government regulation that stifles competition.

JANUARY 13, 1979

If we stand together, if we keep faith with our two centuries of tradition, and if we keep faith with ourselves, then we can achieve a richer quality of life and a new standard of social justice for all Americans.

JUNE 13, 1975

THE MIRACLE
OF 1787

It is not by accident that America over the years has been able to combine the wisdom of Athens and the might of Sparta. We have been a nation thrice blessed —blessed once with abundant natural resources; blessed a second time with a resourceful and stubborn citizenry, who took the nation westward to the Pacific in the nineteenth century and upward to the moon in the twentieth; and blessed a third time with a system of self-government that has reconciled, perhaps more perfectly than any other nation in history, the aspirations of individual freedom with the requirements of social order.

APRIL 30, 1979

As a nation, we have no hereditary institutions, and a minimum of ceremonial symbols. The Constitution itself is our national symbol—the symbol of our identity, our continuity, our unity and also our diversity.

It requires a mature people, mature in intelligence and political understanding, to respect that kind of abstract symbol, rather than the more tangible or human symbols of other nations.

Few, if any, of the great milestones in the history of democracy stand taller than the American Constitution.

The miracle of 1787 was not unprecedented in its larger vision. The constitutional ideas of equality of citizens, protection of minorities, diffusion of the powers of government, and the desire for a fundamental written law are as old as Magna Carta and as current as the Equal Rights Amendment.

21

Our constitutional form of government has demonstrated a formidable ability to respond to challenges from any source—whether from the militant rivalry of totalitarian governments, or from the more friendly competition of parliamentary democracies, or even from the challenge from within by those in high places who would corrupt our system to their own advantage.

Again and again over the past two centuries, the Constitution has proved its capacity to protect and expand our liberty, while safeguarding the domestic order and the national security essential if liberty is to grow and flourish.

SEPTEMBER 22, 1978

History teaches that neither this nor any other generation of Americans can long afford to sleep upon its freedoms. The technocratic society we have today would manage the world and plan it for our good. But that society all too easily views dissent as interference, democracy as frustration, free speech as unaffordable luxury. The Founding Fathers understood that the natural tendency of government is to repress dissent, and to seek order at the price of liberty. They gave us a Constitution and a Bill of Rights to resist these trends and keep us free.

JUNE 13, 1978

Freedom of the press is the cornerstone of our democracy. No reporter should have to go to jail for defending the First Amendment. No editor should be forced to take a lie-detector test at the whim of a disgruntled plaintiff in a libel suit. No publisher should be the victim of large fines for defending his editors and reporters or his basic right to publish.

APRIL 30, 1979

The great recent social and political conflicts of our own generation—the civil-rights movement, the struggle to end the war in Vietnam, the response to Watergate—depended for their success on a free press and the exercise of free speech. What we were, what we are, and what we shall be as a nation and as individuals are closely bound up with that single, simple phrase "Congress shall make no law abridging the freedom of speech."

JUNE 13, 1978

We need more effective safeguards to ensure that every American can fully exercise his constitutional right to privacy. We must protect American citizens against the compiling of inaccurate or unverified data and the unrestricted use and dissemination of such data.

The past several decades have seen an enormous growth in the volume of unregulated information about American citizens. When people apply for insurance, purchase a home, seek employment, acquire a credit card, or act in thousands of other everyday situations, they are evaluated in large part on the basis of information contained in computer data banks. This information is often incomplete, inaccurate, or based upon unverified or hearsay representations. Experience has shown that as the capacity to store and disseminate personal information has increased through the use of computers and other devices, information has been collected to fill this capacity, to the detriment of the right to privacy.

JUNE 12, 1974

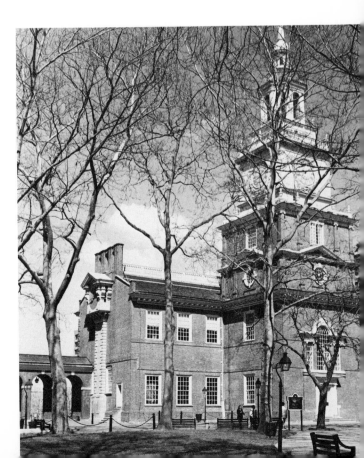

There is not a single institution described in the Constitution which functions today precisely as the framers intended. Nor could they have envisaged the circumstances of twentieth-century America—rising from depression to world power, wealthy beyond their imagination, burdened with unparalleled responsibilities. However, the enormity of change is also a measure of their achievement. For their understanding of public power and its dangers to democracy is as true today as it was in 1787. And it is our departure from that understanding which threatens to erode our freedom.

MAY 14, 1978

I regard the current drive for a constitutional convention as an ominous development for the nation and a serious threat to the integrity of the Constitution. For sound and sufficient reasons, the convention method has never been used before, and it should not be used today.

The great danger of the current convention approach is that its single-minded focus is too narrow to deal with a specific issue like the federal budget deficit in the context of all the other problems that affect it. By contrast, Congress, working properly, is better able to deal with related issues of spending for national defense, health and education, welfare and other questions that must be answered if the federal budget is to be responsibly controlled.

The call for a convention is unwise for another reason. On issues where amendments have been suggested in recent years—such as school busing, abortion, school prayer, or reapportionment—the proponents could not achieve their goal except by amending the Constitution. But it is not necessary to take this step to achieve the goal of a balanced budget. Congress, acting by simple statute, can legislate a balanced budget or reduce the federal deficit. We should not lightly amend the Constitution when other less difficult routes are available to reach the destination.

There are wiser ways in which the Constitution, originally conceived to establish a minimal form of national government, can be made more relevant to the challenge of mastering a government that has become pervasive in our lives.

SEPTEMBER 22, 1978

24

I hope that between now and the bicentennial of 1987, people in towns and communities across the country will meet to discuss and search out ways of restoring the constitutional balance—to distribute authority and responsibility without sacrificing the rights of any of our fellow citizens. The Constitution is still our guide.

MAY 14, 1978

PEOPLE ARE NOT ASKING MUCH FROM GOVERNMENT

It is responsiveness that people seek. Government that is sensitive to the requests of the elderly confused by procedures and forms and carbon copies; sensitive to the commuter sweltering in his car on an expressway; sensitive to the worker who does not want to be laid off in the name of some fiscal policy; sensitive to the consumer who is bilked in his credit; sensitive to the young couple who may never find a mortgage or afford the interest. Government that is interested less in itself and its procedures, and more in the tranquility of its people.

JUNE 12, 1970

The challenge we face today at home and overseas is not primarily a struggle with arms and bombs and tanks and planes against a threat without. Instead, the challenge is a different threat, a threat that comes from within. The weapons are principles and ideas. And the most serious injuries are self-inflicted wounds.

The struggle is for the conscience of America, for a government that is genuinely responsive to the people's need, for a policy that recognizes the true interests of the nation at home and overseas.

MAY 17, 1975

Within Western society today perhaps the universal and overwhelming source of discontent arises from the increasing dehumanization of life. There is a sense of powerlessness, not simply among the young but among all who feel that their lives are spent impersonally in modern societies. More and more, the things that vitally affect us do not submit to control. The institutions created to support us in meeting the responsibilities of our lives—whether religious, political, or educational—no longer respond to the individual's changing needs. The machines of society take on a life of their own. They run themselves, perhaps efficiently, perhaps productively, but seemingly with less and less concern for the desires of the individual human being they were designed to serve.

MARCH 3, 1970

As public affairs become more centralized, as personal and local responsibilities are absorbed, the individual's confidence in himself—in his mastery over the conditions of his own life—has been eroded. Our ability to influence decisions which determine the conditions of daily life is less than it was in America's first generation. And the consequence of this sense of futility is to turn people inward, making them anxious to protect themselves against the uncontrollable future, and depriving us of the energy and confidence which can alone resolve our difficulties.

MAY 14, 1978

For all their hard work and successful efforts in the building of America, the blue-collar workers of this country asked little in return. They did not ask for leisure or luxury. They did not ask for free rides or special privileges. They did not ask for subsidized martinis in their lunch pails. They asked only that the promise of America should be kept. They asked only a fair chance to practice their trade; a fair chance to support their families; a fair chance to make their way in life without unwarranted intrusion by their management or their government.

Their ancestors and mine who reached these shores, the immigrants who built this country and made it great, the Germans and the Poles, the Irish and the Jews and the Italians—none of them landed in America looking for a handout. Brick by brick, stone by stone, generation by generation, they worked hard to earn the promise of America. They brought the American dream closer to reality for their children and themselves.

APRIL 23, 1979

The challenges we face will require important changes in the structure of our institutions. It will not be easy to fit these changes into old categories—liberal or conservative, radical or reactionary. Instead they will bring to our public life new meanings for old words in our political dialogue—words such as "power," "community," "purpose." Power so that individual citizens can regain control over the conditions of their social existence. Community so that individuals can live and work in some kind of shared partnership with their fellow citizens. Purpose so that Americans can feel the pride of participation in a society whose goals are touched with nobility and moral purpose.

MAY 14, 1978

Society's dissatisfactions with too much government are often translated into dissatisfaction with the people in government. This is both understandable and proper. The challenge to those who serve in government is to rethink the role of government; to update what is outmoded; to improve what is inadequate; to discard what is unnecessary; and to soften what is oppressive.

MAY 11, 1977

28

The challenge to improve government is not a new one for America, but today it has special urgency. Like the farmers at Concord Bridge, the embattled taxpayers of California have now fired a shot heard round the world. No person in public life—no president, no senator, no governor, no mayor—can ignore the message and the outraged feelings of the people. Our job is to understand the meaning of Proposition 13 and to carry out its mandate wisely, so that it becomes an effective warning shot across the bow of government, and not a shot below the waterline of the American ship of state. We all are beginning to realize that our resources are limited, that government money cannot be spread without end across the range of problems.

JUNE 19, 1978

The old debate about "states' rights" and "big government" was a contest to decide whether public resources should be used to solve social problems. That battle has been resolved. Injustice and economic decline, the health of our citizens, and the deterioration of our cities are public problems which require public solutions. The challenge now is to find paths toward solutions which do not begin and end in Washington.

MAY 14, 1978

29

Too often in recent years, we have allowed debates on major issues to be polarized beyond the point of no return. We cannot afford to let bad debate drive out the good.

NOVEMBER 2, 1975

To do nothing, to be silent, not to inquire, not to challenge, is to abdicate citizen responsibility. To adopt the code words and catch phrases and epithets of others as personal policy is to substitute reflex for thought. It is no excuse for an informed and literate citizen to claim that leaders have better or secret information, and thus forgo the right to hold a different opinion. In the first place, it is just not so. On most issues all the relevant information is public. In the second place, the issues today really are issues of values, standards, and ideals. On these matters the views of every single citizen are as valid and as informed as those of men in power. And the most troublesome questions confronting Americans do not have Republican answers or Democratic answers or Northern answers or Southern answers. They have human answers, and American answers, for they are the questions that ask what kind of life we want to have.

MAY 30, 1970

To a person in public life, nothing is more distressing today than the massive cynicism, hostility, and outright distrust that is undermining the people's basic faith and confidence in government and its institutions.

SEPTEMBER 10, 1976

Things are not the way they are by accident or chance. Every law that should be repealed, every regulation that should be modified, is on the books today because it benefits an entrenched and powerful interest group that will fight with tooth and claw to keep its special privilege.

JUNE 14, 1979

The time has come to apply the principle of public financing to Congressional elections.

JUNE 6, 1973

Representative government on Capitol Hill is in the worst shape I have seen it in my sixteen years in the Senate. The heart of the problem is that the Senate and the House of Representatives are awash in a sea of special-interest campaign contributions and special-interest lobbying.

OCTOBER 23, 1978

Vast unseen resources are spent by special-interest groups anxious to win the rich favors that government can bestow. Vast underground rivers of influence money quietly seep into the foundation of our system of representative government.

AUGUST 2, 1977

Members of Congress cannot live by political-action committees alone.

APRIL 30, 1979

Public financing of elections is the wisest possible investment that American taxpayers can make in the future of their country.

MAY 5, 1977

Rarely, if ever, in our history have private-interest groups been better organized, better financed, or more resistant to the force of change. It was Lord Bryce who commented in the nineteenth century that American government was all engine and no brakes. Today it could be said, in view of the impasse over energy and many other issues, that our government is all brakes and no engine.

SEPTEMBER 22, 1978

The rise of compact single-issue interest groups and their tactics of non-negotiable demands on politicians are two of the most alarming trends in modern politics. They threaten to dispel the atmosphere of compromise and conciliation in which our system must function if we are to advance the public interest in a way that reconciles the diversity of our people.

No agency of government, no private-interest group, can responsibly afford to

31

press its raw power to the limit. When that occurs, as in Vietnam or Watergate or the court-packing effort of the 1930s, strong counterpressures inevitably arise. They threaten the fabric of society and jeopardize the fragile balance of forces that has always been the real source of America's vitality and strength.

SEPTEMBER 22, 1978

Part of the larger challenge we face is that Congress is a crisis-oriented institution, with few mechanisms and little inclination to deal with problems before they become acute. Every business person understands the importance of the current bottom line. Farmers are understandably anxious about their current harvests. But farmers also understand the importance of sowing now for future years. Executives ask where they want their enterprises to be next year or farther in the future.

In our complex, interdependent and rapidly changing world, we need a similar approach to public policy. We need better distant early-warning signals, better mechanisms and institutional arrangements for handling problems which are not yet brush fires, but which are already smoldering and may well cause the conflagrations of the future.

APRIL 30, 1979

The answer is to make America work. And the way to make America work is to roll up our sleeves and make government itself begin to work responsibly. If we succeed, we shall be able to hand down to our children and future generation the same great nation our ancestors handed down to us.

OCTOBER 18, 1978

In taking up the mantle of public service, we become participants, not spectators, in shaping the great goals of our community, state and nation. We are sworn to the service of all the people—not just the few who are rich and powerful, but also the many others whom we serve, and for whom we are so often the only voice they have.

JANUARY 24, 1974

Why shouldn't those who pay exorbitant prices for drugs and who rely on them for their daily well-being be represented as well as drug manufacturers?

Why shouldn't parents of children attending federally assisted schools be heard alongside representatives of local governments?

Why shouldn't airline, bus, and railway passengers be heard as well as the airlines, the bus companies and the railways?

32

Why shouldn't those who breathe polluted air, who are displaced or annoyed by freeways, and who buy and drive automobiles be heard as well as the automobile manufacturers and the concrete industry?

Why shouldn't the purchasers and viewers of television sets be heard as well as the networks and the station owners?

Why aren't construction workers consulted as well as contractors about federal or federally assisted projects?

Why isn't the interest of the housewife in providing wholesome and reasonably priced food for her family represented in addition to the food wholesalers and manufacturers in relevant agency proceedings?

Who speaks for the disabled veteran, the widow, the elderly when proposed federal action will affect their security?

JULY 21, 1970

People today are not asking much from government. They are asking for the simple things that make a difference in their lives—things that people have sought in this country ever since the first settlers landed on our shores. They want jobs where they can work, not lines at the local welfare or unemployment office. They want prices at the supermarket their budgets can afford. They want schools that can bring their children a decent education. They want health care to be a basic right for all, not just an expensive privilege for the few. They want safe streets where they can walk at night, instead of barricading their homes against the rising tide of crime. They want other important things that can make a difference in their lives.

OCTOBER 14, 1976

Policy formation without public participation is like faith and hope without charity. And public-interest groups cannot possibly participate in competition with special-interest groups unless they have adequate financing.

JUNE 3, 1975

The challenge is to develop a modern and realistic role for government, a role that will be as responsive to the nation's needs as government used to be during our finest moments of the past. These moments did not grow out of excessive caution, but out of a boldness and willingness to experiment with new solutions and new approaches. We must go forward even if we occasionally do falter.

AUGUST 28, 1978

ENVIRONMENT AND ENERGY

Just a few decades ago Americans were looking for more oil, uranium, and gold; we were building larger buildings and increasing the productivity of our farms and industries. We looked upon land and water as another possible natural resource to be developed—and exploited.

Now our attention has turned back to the primary elements. Frantically we search for clean air, clear water, and unscarred land. As we do so, we find ourselves looking back to the ancient ideal and understanding that man has a special relationship with his land and water and air. People are beginning to realize that we are part of nature, not outside it. We are beginning to understand that instead of conquering nature we must live in harmony with it.

JANUARY 26, 1970

What is striking about America today is that regardless of income, all of us are losing control over the quality of our lives. None of us can run away from air pollution, water pollution, and noise pollution. None of us can escape shoddy and unsafe products.

SEPTEMBER 24, 1970

There is a new awareness that environmental protection is not inconsistent with individual property rights; that government at all levels has an essential

role to play in that protection; and that preservation
of our natural resources is in the individual interest,
as well as for the general good of the public.
NOVEMBER 4, 1973

We need new and imaginative solutions to the very
thorny problem of preserving and protecting fragile
lands from the pressures of haphazard development.
MAY 20 1973

There is a recognition throughout the nation that it will take a unified, coordinated
and enormous effort to bring about the sweeping kinds of changes needed to
protect the unique areas of this country.

The benefits of this protection will be adequate and clean water supplies, rec-
reational areas, wildlife and preservation areas, scenic and aesthetic values, and
an assurance that devastating overdevelopment will not ultimately run dry the
economy of a region.
NOVEMBER 4, 1973

35

Last Tuesday, the landscape architects took down one of the great monuments on the Capitol grounds, the magnificent English elm that had stood watch for so many years over the walk between the Capitol and the Russell Senate Office Building.

They said that the tree had become infected by Dutch elm disease, that it came out in full foliage this spring but died suddenly, and that it had to be removed quickly because of the danger of infection of other trees. Trees that large are impossible to save, they said, and the efforts that were made were unsuccessful. They counted 110 annual rings, and estimated that the tree dated back at least to the early years after the Civil War.

Few if any trees anywhere were better known or more loved by members of the Senate. As we walked to the Capitol from the Russell Building, we passed under its giant limb, a cantilevered miracle of nature that stretched out across the sidewalk and over the roadway. Often we would reach up to touch the limb, or give it a warm slap of recognition and appreciation for its enduring vigil.

President Kennedy, when he was a senator, liked to call it the Humility Tree, because senators instinctively ducked or bowed their heads as they approached the limb and passed beneath it.

The records are dim about its origin. But those of us who enjoyed the beauty of this elm can be grateful to the ancestors who planted it long ago. For a century, it graced the grounds of the Capitol of our growing nation. We could, perhaps, brighten these grounds for posterity to come, by planting a successor worthy of the giant that has fallen. Perhaps, when it falls, in its turn, a century from now, that future generation of the Senate will pause, as we pause today, and know we cared.

JUNE 27, 1978

We face the alarming possibility that among the enormous number of substances that our highly industrialized society is spewing into the environment are some that even now may be causing massive cancer epidemics for the next generation of Americans. We are in the impossible position of walking through a mine field blindfolded, with the knowledge that the devices we trigger today may not explode until our children walk through that field a generation from now.

FEBRUARY 15, 1978

Our fish and marine resources are in jeopardy. Our stocks of haddock, herring, menhaden, flounder, cod and lobster are threatened. Our coastal fishing industry faces the loss of its livelihood if the depletion of these resources continues.

The two-hundred-mile limit we seek is not designed to take the place of international negotiation, but to encourage effective and enforceable agreements. It is not designed to hamper relations between nations, but to foster goodwill among all maritime nations which participate in the world fishing industry. It is not designed to build walls around our country, but to encourage a reasoned and sensible approach to the conservation of the world's marine resources which are vital to all peoples of the globe. It is not designed to be a permanent solution to a difficult problem, but a temporary measure to assure that when all the negotiations are finished, there will be fish and marine resources left for the world to share.

MAY 14, 1974

We cannot shirk our responsibility for the resources of the oceans. It is our duty to lead the other maritime nations of the world into recognition of the growing problem, and to develop more effective methods of cooperation in meeting the need for conservation of these resources. We ask all the nations of the world to join with us as guardians and protectors of the ocean's resources for the benefit of all generations to come.

MAY 14, 1974

Energy conservation is our most undeveloped energy resource. Estimates of the energy that is needlessly wasted in the United States are mind-boggling.

The more efficient use of energy is the least expensive, most environmentally safe, and quickest way to increase energy supplies.

FEBRUARY 25, 1976

For too long we have allowed energy policy to be made by the producers for the consumers. For too long, energy policy has been made at the wellhead and in the board rooms of the industry, instead of in the living rooms of the consumers.

We must balance the millions of dollars of the energy companies with the voices of millions of Americans demanding justice on energy policy.

JANUARY 27, 1978

The nuclear-reactor accident at Three Mile Island raises serious questions about the future of nuclear power. But it also raises even larger questions about what sort of overall approach we are taking in this country to the critical problem of energy. We need a comprehensive risk-assessment approach, not just for nuclear energy, but for all the other sources of energy. We know that nuclear energy has major risks that are of obvious concern to public health and safety. But coal has risks, too, particularly in relation to air quality. Oil has separate but equally enormous risks, especially the danger of a future embargo and its effect on our national security. We have to do a better job of weighing these risks and measuring the costs and benefits and deciding the direction we want to go. We can't just cross our fingers or bury our heads in the sand. We need a national discussion and debate on each of these dimensions of the energy crisis.

APRIL 19, 1979

Is coal safer than nuclear power because it cannot have catastrophic accidents? Or is nuclear power safer than coal because its routine operation does not poison the air?

MAY 31, 1979

America is fortunate that, even after thirty years of development, nuclear power now provides less than four percent of our energy needs. In the past fifteen months, serious safety problems have forced the shutdown of fifteen of the seventy-one operating reactors. If the nation had been heavily committed to nuclear power, such a shutdown could have been a disaster for our economy.

The nuclear-safety licensing process is not working. The dream of nuclear power has become a nightmare of nuclear fear. If we cannot assure the people of this country that the problem of nuclear wastes can be solved, and that serious accidents and massive releases of radioactivity from nuclear power plants can be prevented, then the era of nuclear power is over in the United States.

A national reassessment is under way to determine whether any additional commitments to nuclear power should be made. The question is not whether to build nuclear power plants quickly. Unless we can build them safely, they should not be built at all.

MAY 6, 1979

We need a greater national commitment to solar energy—involving not only research and development related to the scientific and technical aspects of such energy, but also efforts to develop the mechanisms to move these technologies into the commercial marketplace.

This nation has the resources and the talent to achieve the widespread commercial utilization of solar energy in all sectors of our economy.

OCTOBER 8, 1975

For the poor and middle-income Americans throughout the country the situation has gotten worse, not better. Fourteen million Americans pay twenty-five percent of their budget for energy alone. In major Northern cities those at or under the poverty level last winter paid more than forty-five percent of their income for energy, according to the National Center for Community Action. "Let them freeze in the dark" has become not just a clever cliché but a cruel reality.

In this situation, three things seem clear to me: First, we must halt the soaring increases in the price of oil. Second, we must establish inflation guidelines for energy, just like other items in the economy. Third, we must find ways to protect those who are most vulnerable to the price increases that have already taken place.

Incredibly, we have failed to use our funds, our technology, and our diplomacy to increase oil exploration and development in Latin America and Africa. We are sitting on our hands when we should be searching for new oil sources to compete with OPEC. Instead of promoting pessimistic reports that turn out to be exaggerated, we should be working to make the optimistic potential a reality.

JANUARY 9, 1979

Major new pools of oil are waiting to be discovered in unexplored far-flung corners of the world. We have barely begun to make the effort. We have drilled more holes in Arkansas in search of oil than in all of Latin America, more holes in North America than in the rest of the world combined.

MAY 12, 1979

The United States has failed to devise any coherent policy on Mexican oil and gas. Surely that is a major failure in both our energy policy and our foreign policy.

JANUARY 30, 1979

The most effective solution to our energy crisis can be summed up in two words, the words that built this country and made it great, the words that symbolize the backbone of our economy: free enterprise. We can build greater competition into our domestic market, so that alternative energy sources and more efficient uses of energy will emerge as quickly as they can be developed by the ingenuity of a vigorous American free-enterprise system.

We need not fear the actions of the OPEC nations. We can place our trust and reliance on a better system, our system of free enterprise—a system in which numerous energy sources at home and overseas compete to supply our nation's energy needs.

MAY 12, 1979

CITY AND FARM

When cities first evolved thousands of years ago, they met the needs of their citizens. They provided protection from marauders, proximity for trade, transportation and communication, and a common cultural experience which their citizens could enjoy.

MAY 7, 1978

Statistics often hide the individual faces of despair. We don't need statistics to demonstrate the problem. We have seen their faces. We know better than most the profound unfairness of poverty amidst our wealth and technology. Some 3.6 million American families live in overcrowded housing. Over sixty percent of our families can't afford the median-priced home. One out of five Americans is illiterate. Over forty percent of black youth in Boston don't have jobs. Six hundred thousand people in Massachusetts have no health insurance; yet here in this commonwealth, a single day in a hospital costs over two hundred dollars.

NOVEMBER 3, 1977

It seems that we have lost hold of our communities. It seems as though our country is pulling apart into separate peoples who do not know one another. Separate societies of rich and poor, white and black, old and young, urban and rural. Where whites have jobs and blacks have unemployment, where the middle class lives in suburbs and the poor are left in the ghettos, where one group of Americans looks upon another group of Americans with growing mistrust, and even dread.

44

And where, not because we lack the goodwill, but because we lack the faith in ourselves, our response often is to bolt the door, hire more police, and stay as far away from centers of violence as possible.

APRIL 5, 1968

Let us honor those responsible for bringing green space into our urban centers. It is as difficult to imagine New York City without its Central Park as to think of Boston without the Emerald Necklace sweeping along the Charles River through the Fenway, across Jamaica Pond to Franklin Park. Every day, each of us in Congress has an opportunity to enjoy the landscape around the Capitol. Often, we take the simple beauty of the grounds for granted. But all of us at different moments are struck by their quiet, peaceful charm and grace.

MAY 1, 1979

The quality of the life of our cities ultimately will determine the future of America. The struggle for the future of our cities is critical. It is a struggle that affects our lives and the lives of our children. It is a struggle that we are capable of winning, a struggle that we have the resources to win.

JULY 7, 1975

We can make our cities citadels of the human spirit, proud beacons of hope in a prosperous and democratic land.

JANUARY 1, 1976

Never has there been a greater gulf between the problems of the cities and the comforts of the suburbs. As the gap grows wider, the cities have been left with fewer resources to resolve their problems. They are losing the resource of people, because as suburbs grow, the cities have declined in population. They are losing the resource of dollars, because as industry moves out, the property base dries up and revenues decline.

JUNE 19, 1978

We must halt the government policies that tend to destroy or subvert the neighborhoods and central cities in which our people live. It is a policy of violent death that makes handguns readily available for those who use our city streets for crime. It is a policy of slow death that allows businesses to be driven out of the cities to the beltways and shopping centers of the suburbs. It is a policy of absurdity that allows community-development grants to be spent on new sewer systems in suburban developments, rather than to replace the aging water mains in our cities.

MAY 7, 1978

No one can mistake the neglect in the fiscal crisis that robs cities of tax revenues and then demands additional social services that cannot be afforded without new debt. The victims have been the elderly poor, the black, the Chicano, the inner-city youth—and the battlefields have been the centers of our cities.

JUNE 11, 1976

So much of our heritage and so much of our future depend upon our countryside. It is not merely that rural residents provide us with our most necessary commodity —though they provide the food which sustains us. It is not merely that they provide us with billions of dollars in other goods and services—though they provide items for every facet of our lives.

Rural America is vital because it provides us with much more than that. Our small towns and farms embody the independence of spirit, the sense of responsibility, the commitment to community, which are at the core of our national strength.

JUNE 25, 1979

We all understand the vital role the farmer plays in our economy and around the world; yet it is incredible to me that this great country cannot develop a farm policy that guarantees an adequate supply of food for every citizen and a fair return for every farmer. It is bad enough that the farmer has to worry about what the weather may do to his crops, but he shouldn't also have to worry about what the government is also doing to him. America's national pie is big enough for all of us to share. Rich and poor, business and labor, farmer and consumer, we are all in this together.

MAY 27, 1976

It is the farmer who is squeezed the most by the breakdown of the country's economy. The consumers of Massachusetts cannot prosper if the farmers of North Dakota do not prosper.

NOVEMBER 6, 1971

Year by year, we see more farmland turned into more parking lots. Year by year, we see more farms lost in our economy. Haphazard zoning, uncontrolled development, highway construction, and urban sprawl—all too often the victim has been our best farmland. And once those acres are lost, they are lost forever. You cannot replace prime farmland.

AUGUST 27, 1976

We have a tremendous potential to produce food sufficient for our own needs and sufficient to help alleviate the growing food crisis around the world. We need a comprehensive food policy that provides reasonable prices to consumers along with legitimate income protection for farmers. We need a food policy that doesn't pay farmers not to produce. We need a reserve program to ensure market stability during periods of shortage and surplus. We must stop denying ourselves and the poor the benefit of our agricultural technology.

FEBRUARY 9, 1977

Conglomerates are literally swallowing the best and most promising lands and farms in this country. We need to strengthen the efficient family farmer and not the conglomerate agribusiness looking for places to store its excess funds. We need to let the people who live on the land decide how their land will be developed.

JUNE 25, 1979

We need more effective land-use planning. There are thousands of young people who love farming. We must give them a chance. We have to restore a belief in the importance of farming.

AUGUST 27, 1976

A farmer earns less today for a bushel of wheat than he did a generation ago. He pays more for seed, he pays more for machinery, he pays more for freight. And he finds his income shrinking year by year. Neither plague nor drought nor natural disaster could have damaged the American farmer as much as the indifferent policy of recent years.

NOVEMBER 6, 1971

It has been said that a farmer is typically a person whose assets are in property and whose liabilities are in money. He lives poor and dies rich.

That formula will not keep American agriculture flourishing. The evidence is substantial that many farmers feel they are an endangered species. The number of farms in this country has dropped from six million after World War II to less than three million today. In Massachusetts, the number has plunged from 35,000 to 6,000. Less than a third of the nation's farmers receive the majority of their income from their farms.

The problem is not caused by inefficiency. Never before have so few produced so much for so many as do American farmers today. They provide food for their 200 million fellow citizens. And then they produce as much food again for billions of peoples in other lands. They are ever willing to work the long hours, to learn the new techniques, to face the awesome challenge of providing the sustenance by which others live and thrive.

And yet the farmer is unfairly vulnerable. He is vulnerable because of huge fluctuations in prices, vulnerable because he must go deeply into debt today but will not learn the value of his crop until some distant future, vulnerable to myriad other events he is unable to control.

We need a policy that does not set our farmers adrift on waves of price fluctuations from one year to the next. We need a policy that guarantees to farmers a fair return for their labors and their harvests. We need a policy that preserves our family farms and halts the unfair speculation that drives up the price of land. We need a policy that attracts young people into farming and enables American men and women to farm with greater confidence than they have today. Only in this way can all our other citizens continue to enjoy the benefits of an abundant and vigorously competitive farm sector. Only in this way can our vaunted American system of agriculture continue to be the envy of the world.

JUNE 7, 1979

51

HUMAN RIGHTS BEGIN AT HOME

America's heritage rests upon the noble vision that
all persons are created equal.

JANUARY 26, 1976

The American people care deeply about human
rights around the world. But they also believe that
human rights begin at home.

JUNE 9, 1977

No nation can afford the waste of its citizens. No
nation can afford to assign a group of people to the
fringes of existence. Only when the conditions of
misery and injustice that breed hatred and despair
are challenged will we achieve reconciliation.

SEPTEMBER 19, 1977

The survival of the strong and the success of the fortunate cannot blind us to the
plight of the weak and the failure of the unlucky. No Americans should have to
be born into a world where they can succeed only if their strength is greater,
where they can prevail only if their endurance is longer, where they can advance
only if their luck is better than that required of the rest of us.

The great unmentioned problem of America today is the growth, rapid and
insidious, of a group in our midst, perhaps more dangerous, more bereft of hope,
more difficult to confront, than any for which our history has prepared us. It is a

52

group that threatens to become what America has never known—a permanent underclass in our society.

You know who they are, as do we all. They are the millions who have been left behind and show no signs of catching up. They are the casualties who huddle in the center of the great cities. They are our shame. And they are our brothers and sisters. They are the cancer of the American soul.

They are the other side, the untold side, of the statistics of our progress. The improvement of life for many, and the remarkable achievements of some, cannot obscure the fact that for others these past years have represented, not advancing hope, but degradation and disintegration of an almost apocalyptic degree.

This story is a monumental tragedy of modern American life. It is a silent story, but it is the ominous silence of a time bomb ticking inside the heart of America.

MAY 7, 1978

Today, just a few short years from the celebration of our two hundredth year in existence, the Spanish-speaking community in this land finds irony rather than solace in the protections of the Bill of Rights.

As a nation, we have marveled at the bounty of our farms. But we have overlooked the men and women who toil in the dust and dirt to harvest that bounty.

As a nation, we have been silent partners in the denial of the constitutional right to an equal education for millions of Spanish-speaking children in our schools.

As a nation, we have forgotten that if the Chicanos are angry and alienated, it is we, the majority, who have made them strangers in their own land.

This nation can never be completely free nor completely whole until we know that no child cries from hunger in the Rio Grande Valley, until we know that no mother in East Los Angeles lives in terror of illness in her family because she cannot afford a doctor, until we know that no men or women or children suffer because the law refuses to recognize their humanity.

It is not for the Chicano alone that we seek these goals. It is not for the disadvantaged alone that we seek these goals. It is for America's future.

JULY 27, 1972

53

The legal issues affecting the Spanish-speaking and other ethnic minorities do not end with the administration of justice or equal educational opportunity. They span virtually every area where society and the individual interact. In public and private employment, in immigration, in housing, in farm labor, in health, in political participation—in all of these areas, there is need for examination of the legal status of the Spanish-speaking. In all of these areas there is too much left undone as the nation seeks to redeem its commitment to equal justice.

MAY 1, 1975

54

Boston Harbor brought the poor to a rich land, and the land gave her riches to our ancestors. Who is to say this chain should now be broken? Who dares assert that some shall be forever poor? Such thoughts are foreign to those of us who came from immigrant faith.

To those who say hold off, to those who would slow the advance of others, I say the problem is not that easy to escape. Cover the mineshaft, but the fires will rage below. Flee from this grave problem now and you will leave it for your children and their children. All deserve to share the fruits of progress. We withhold them at our peril, and at the peril of the society we love.

JUNE 12, 1970

Is it fair that a child's future in Appalachia is limited to the hollows that his father and his father before him have struggled to escape?

Is it fair that a child growing up black in the ghettos of our cities is more likely to drop out of high school than to graduate from college?

Is it fair that a child should know no home except the current migratory-labor camp?

Is it fair that a child born on an Indian reservation may not see a doctor for the first six years of his life?

Is it fair that any child's future should be limited by the color of his skin, or the Spanish lilt to his name, or the sharing of an Indian heritage?

JANUARY 26, 1976

True, the District of Columbia has no vast farmlands or natural resources. But, as the Supreme Court ruled over a decade ago, it is people who vote, not acres or trees. The District has its share of painters and plumbers, bakers and carpenters, engineers and electricians, shoe stores and grocery stores, florists and laundries, movie theaters and hospitals, colleges and museums, and a panorama of other occupations and activities found in the fifty states.

The District has a population greater than six states; its citizens pay more federal taxes than in eleven states; and more D.C. sons lost their lives in the Vietnam War than did those of ten states.

It is unfair to hold the citizens of the District hostage to the prevailing antigovernment mood. Congress and the states must find effective ways to deal with the legitimate national concerns about the size of government, the level of government spending, and the degree of government regulation in our lives. But there are better ways to reach these legitimate ends than by the illegitimate means of discriminating against the hundreds of thousands of ordinary private American citizens who live and work and make their homes in the nation's capital. They deserve the same right that all other citizens enjoy—the right to representation in their government, the right to elect their own members of the United States Senate and the House of Representatives.

FEBRUARY 26, 1979

Our task is to restore America's fundamental commitment to human rights and human values. This is what our country is all about. We can achieve a society where a child's future does not rest on whether he is born white or black, Chicano or Irish, Jew or Catholic. That day will come. That is the promise of America. It is a promise we must keep.

JANUARY 1, 1976

Historians of the future will wonder about the years we have just passed through. They will ask how it could be, a century after the Civil War, that black and white had not yet learned to live together in the promise of this land.

JANUARY 26, 1976

Perhaps the most difficult challenge the nation faces—more difficult than any other challenge of foreign or domestic policy—is the unfinished business of the Constitution and the Civil War: the task of achieving peace and equality between the races in our society.

AUGUST 1, 1978

We are going to capture Jericho. And we shall do it with a coalition of black and white, Democrats and Republicans, North and South, old and young.

And when our trumpet sounds, those walls of oppression and discrimination and injustice will come tumbling down. And on that day, we shall have a new America, one nation, indivisible, with liberty and justice for all.

SEPTEMBER 30, 1978

While economic growth is important for all Americans, it is absolutely essential for black Americans. It is the indispensable condition of black progress. Other groups may have achieved a level of comfort satisfactory to themselves. But they have no right to stop the engines of growth before others have begun to board the train.

MAY 7, 1978

It is a stain on our democracy that the life expectancy of black Americans is five years lower than in the nation as a whole, or that the life expectancy of a migrant worker is forty-nine, compared to the average of seventy-three for all Americans. It is a stain on our democracy that infant mortality is fifty to a hundred percent higher in urban ghettos than in the nation as a whole.

MAY 7, 1978

There is a common good, a common thread of humanity, that draws us together. We cannot ignore our opportunities nor hide from our responsibilities. What diminishes our fellow human beings diminishes ourselves as well.

If we seek justice for ourselves, then we must demand it for others. If we seek equality for ourselves, than we must demand it for others. For none of us will enjoy the precious fruits of our heritage in the future unless all of us enjoy them together. It will take both blacks and whites together to chart a new course for America.

MAY 27, 1977

We must pledge to rekindle the spirit of peace and justice that is the enduring legacy of Dr. Martin Luther King, Jr. For Dr. King awakened America. He was the heart of a mighty engine that moved this country toward a new revival of spirit and hope.

His dream guided us when our vision dimmed. His courage inspired us when the sacrifices seemed too great. His ideas guided us when our footsteps faltered. His memory summons us again to action. It sounds the trumpet for new battles, for fresh assaults on the walls of racism and discrimination.

JANUARY 15, 1977

Let us not forget the black women throughout our history who have led their people toward freedom. Let us not forget Rosa Parks, who sat down and forced a nation to stand up. As Fannie Lou Hamer said, "Rosa was just tired of being tired."

Let us not forget the sit-ins, the wade-ins, the freedom rides that unified black Americans' demands for equality.

Let us not forget the years when the churches and congregations, led by the NAACP and many others, rocked to the strains of "We Shall Overcome" and "Ain't Gonna Let Nobody Turn Us Around."

MAY 7, 1978

We owe the people action on equal rights, so that no qualified American is denied a leadership role in business, law, medicine, government, teaching or any other profession because of race or sex.

JUNE 19, 1975

During the past decade, the women's movement has been an effective and significant force in implementing positive social change in this nation. Despite significant progress, however, examination of today's society reveals that, while women comprise fifty-one percent of our population, they are a long way from achieving economic or social equality.

JANUARY 31, 1979

The time has come for this nation to guarantee to the millions of our working women that sex discrimination in employment is ended. The time has come for all of us to understand that the nation's economy and the economic resources and stability of countless families depend to a significant degree on the earnings of women. The time has come to end the ridiculous notion that we can afford to waste, through discrimination, the wealth of talent and energy that women can bring to our nation's work force.

SEPTEMBER 15, 1975

58

The Equal Rights Amendment is going to be ratified. It is going to be ratified because this country cannot preach human rights abroad while over half of our own population is still denied equal rights at home.

OCTOBER 7, 1978

As a symbol of this progress, you may recall the famous photograph of the mountain climber from Japan who became the first woman to climb Mount Everest. Her own success is a symbol of the success of many other women who are climbing Everests of their own in many different fields.

OCTOBER 25, 1978

There has never been a period in American history when the future held more promise for young women. The age-old barriers of sex discrimination are crumbling. At last, the nation is beginning to draw upon the full resources of its women, with potentially great reward for every area of our national and local life. For young women today, the opportunities are especially great. There has never been a better or more hopeful time for a young woman to grow up in the history of our country.

JUNE 4, 1978

After two hundred years, I think it is safe to say that women in America are now demanding full equality in every aspect of American life. And after two hundred years, I think they have every right to expect it. Nor can this nation afford to deny it.

MAY 18, 1976

From time to time in this nation's history, public attention is focused on the American Indian as though he had just arrived on our shores with new problems never before contemplated by government. There is a public cry for action. The wheels of government begin to churn. Congress and the executive branch deliberate, and then issue nice phrases. Finally, the difficulty of the task overwhelms us, our sense of immediacy fades, our indignation wanes, and the Indian "problem" is shelved for another generation.

JULY 12, 1978

Native Americans have long awaited a time when they might determine their own futures. Today, after generations of struggle, their rights of self-determination are being taken seriously. The central focus of Indian self-determination must continue to be maintenance of a firm and secure natural-resource base for tribal economic development. Our efforts, however, must also be focused on a second level; that is, providing basic assistance to the tribes for development of their own internal institutions. Effective Indian self-government through tribal institutions must be a cornerstone of federal policy.

JUNE 14, 1978

On most fronts, our government has failed to fulfill its obligations and responsibilities to protect Indian rights and resources. For the Indian people, our two centuries of national life have, all too often, consisted of battles with the white man, followed by promises which were broken and commitments which remain unfulfilled.

JUNE 22, 1976

The protection of Indian rights will be a long struggle. We must not again ignore the needs of our first Americans. The injustices experienced by American Indians are not just ancient wrongs or broken promises out of our distant past. They are part of the Indian's world today, a world which grinds out new injustices, new indignities, and new wrongs day by day.

I look forward to the day when we see dignity restored to a proud people.

JULY 12, 1978

Not so long ago, when my grandfather, Honey Fitz, was growing up in politics in Massachusetts, he could walk the streets of Boston and see the ads for work that said "No Irish need apply." Those harsh and unacceptable attitudes of religious and ethnic prejudice are largely gone from American life today. And the same sort of change can come for others too. Change can come for women. Change can come for black Americans. Change can come for native Americans. It can come for all those who, in other generations, would have been condemned to live as victims of prejudice and denial of opportunity.

JUNE 4, 1978

60

The ancient Greeks too met challenges that were difficult to conquer. Our two million Americans of Greek descent are rightly proud of their great ancestry. They carry in their own blood the precious heritage of democracy from the place where it was born in Greece more than two thousand years ago.

OCTOBER 17, 1970

You and I and many others have shared too much joy, too much sorrow, too much victory, and too much pain to retreat before the present looming obstacles to freedom, equality and justice.

MAY 7, 1978

Let each of us, to the best of our ability, in our own day and generation, perform something worthy to be remembered.

MARCH 1, 1976

Of course we need a strong defense. But we already have a strong defense. What we also need is an equally strong defense against poverty and disease, against prejudice and lack of education, against crime and slums. These goals are also basic to the real security of America—because, in the last analysis, the only security worth having is the people's faith that the nation is worth securing.

MAY 27, 1977

National security begins at home. It begins on the streets and sidewalks of our cities. It begins in the small towns and villages of our country. It begins on the farms in our rural areas.

These are the places where the first two hundred years of our nation were decided. And these are the places where the fate of America is going to be decided in the third century of our history.

MARCH 1, 1976

Two hundred years of injustice is enough.

APRIL 8, 1976

AN AGE OF LAW,
AN AGE OF JUSTICE

Violence scars our nation and corrupts our young. What does it take to teach America about itself? What does it take to make this country learn? After all we have been through in recent years—the campus violence, the street violence, the handgun violence, the urban violence, the wave of adult crime, the epidemic of juvenile crime, the assaults upon our leaders and even their assassinations—after all of this, can anyone deny that our generation has abdicated its responsibility to tame the violence in our character?

FEBRUARY 12, 1976

Crime in American society is not a new problem. But its recent unchecked growth must be viewed with deep alarm by all law-abiding citizens.

OCTOBER 20, 1975

Responsible programs for crime control have been delayed by the senseless debate over who is tough on crime and who is soft on crime.

NOVEMBER 2, 1975

What is at stake is not whether we are labeled "hard" or "soft" on crime. What is at stake is our competence, our ability to reduce criminal violence in ways that reflect our basic legal values. In any nation suffering from violence, the danger is understandable that the passion for safety and security may override traditional principles and lead to harsh solutions that only make the problems worse. Sometimes, as we learned in the early 1970s, government itself inflames the problem by encouraging simplistic solutions and law-and-order rhetoric. The test for our generation and for the decade of the 1980s is whether we can shed these shibboleths and develop workable alternatives to bring the crime rate down.

JUNE 1, 1979

All is not well in America's house of law. Serious problems undermine the legal system. As new laws and regulations are born, grievances grow geometrically. The courts are choked with litigants. Parties abandon valid legal claims because vindication is not worth the delay and cost. Suits drag on for decades. Criminals on bail commit new crimes before they can be brought to trial. Other criminals go free under dubious plea bargains struck because dockets are too overcrowded and judges and prosecutors are too overworked to go to trial at all.

What we need now and in the years to come is a concerted and systematic effort to streamline our legal system, to strip away the waste and fat, to achieve the goal of meaningful delegalization of America.

That effort does not mean throwing out the baby with the bathwater. It does not mean the wholesale dismantling of measures painfully enacted over many decades to protect the public health and safety and preserve the beauty of our environment.

It does not mean arbitrarily locking the courthouse door to classes of litigants who have not yet won full access to the justice they deserve if their basic American right to life, liberty and the pursuit of happiness is to have meaning in modern life.

What it does mean is an attempt to end the suffocating burden of litigation, delay and red tape that unnecessarily clogs the courts. It means an effort to develop alternative avenues of redress that do not require the cumbersome machinery of judicial resolution of disputes. It means a greater effort to bring order to the chaos of conflicting and overlapping bodies of law like the federal criminal code, so that those charged with crime can be brought to trial, and those convicted can be fairly sentenced.

JUNE 14, 1979

Charles Thompson recently pleaded guilty in New York to manslaughter in the first degree. He shot a cabdriver he was trying to rob when the man put up an unexpected fight.

Before sentencing, the judge received a probation report. Charles Thompson, it seems, has only one leg. He lost the other at Khe Sanh. He also has a heroin addiction that he acquired at an army hospital in Japan. He returned to the United States, as have so many of our veterans, without adequate education or job training, crippled and addicted, without any prospect or hope of employment. His disability pay was inadequate to support his habit. So he did the only thing he was trained to do—he used a gun.

The judge was compassionate. He could not just release this dangerous man. He had to think of the next cabdriver. So he called agency after agency, state and federal and local and private, trying to find any place or person who would accept responsibility for treating Charles Thompson under appropriate safeguards. There was none. No one would take him in. And so, two days before Thanksgiving, Charles Thompson was sentenced to serve up to twenty-five years in Attica State Prison.

JANUARY 17, 1972

The most important way to start is to match our rhetoric with reality. Let us make no irresponsible promises. Let us raise no public expectation that peace on the streets is now at hand, or that reductions in crime can easily be achieved.

We will never rid our streets completely of crime. But we can start in a new and more promising direction than we have tried before. And if we make that start, we shall have a new sense of confidence that we are moving in the right direction. Then, at last, we shall have a reasonable chance of achieving progress in the difficult but still not hopeless war on crime in our society.

OCTOBER 20, 1975

As far back as Justinian's Rome, criminal codes have been symbols of justice, examples of society's commitment to the principle of fairness. In this respect, the current federal criminal code is a disgrace. Congresses over the years have enacted some three thousand criminal laws, piling one on top of another, until we have a structure that looks more like a Rube Goldberg contraption than a comprehensive criminal code. The sad fact is that our current federal criminal law is archaic, unfair, and unacceptably ambiguous.

JANUARY 19, 1978

Criminal-code reform is a massive undertaking, of critical importance to the American people. It is the cornerstone of the federal government's law enforcement policy.

The goals of criminal-code reform are obvious —to simplify the law, make it understandable to the citizen, repeal archaic laws, and add provisions to meet the problems of modern society.

APRIL 2, 1977

When we speak about violent crime, one problem stands out above the rest—the plague of juvenile violence. Juvenile crime is more than a fact of life today; it is a fact of death. The statistics are foreboding. Although juveniles under the age of eighteen constitute only about one fifth of the population, they account for nearly half of those arrested for serious crime. And juvenile violence has been increasing faster then crime generally.

Significant punishment should be imposed on the young offender who commits a violent crime. This should translate into jail in a special juvenile facility for the most serious violent offender; victim restitution, community service, periodic detention or intensive supervision are all promising alternatives for less violent offenders.

OCTOBER 8, 1978

Just as important as any specific law enforcement steps is the need to demolish city slums, end poverty and discrimination, and provide decent health care, education and jobs for all our citizens. We must reinforce and expand the search for social justice in America. Minorities, youths, the uneducated, the unemployed, live in desolation in our inner cities. Absenteeism from schools is tragically high, and unemployment figures even higher. Some welfare programs contribute to the breakdown of poor families, thereby promoting crime. The drug culture fosters crime, especially in ghettos.

NOVEMBER 1, 1976

68

Our current bail procedures are not working. In particular, they pose an unnecessary threat to the safety of the community. It is time to recognize that these procedures need substantial revision, within the scope of what is permissible under the Constitution.

JUNE 1, 1979

The death penalty is wrong in principle, and it is applied in an arbitrary and unfair manner.

MARCH 12, 1974

Let us not confuse social progress with progress in the war on crime. A fair and workable system of law enforcement is a goal we must strive for in and of itself. We delude ourselves if we say, "No crime reform until society is reformed." In every society there will always be those who, whether motivated by greed or anger, perversity or frustration, poverty or intolerance, illness or ignorance, refuse to live in peace with their fellow citizens. We must move beyond the limitations of past debate and remove this threat from our streets.

SEPTEMBER 2, 1976

Crime does not end on the local street corner. Hardly a day goes by without some new disclosure of consumer fraud, government corruption, and tax cheating. White-collar crime, organized crime, and political corruption, although often invisible, have become big business.

The failure to investigate, prosecute and punish the white-collar offender, the organized-crime racketeer, and the corrupt government official leads to a loss of public confidence in the integrity of our political, economic and governmental institutions.

SEPTEMBER 2, 1976

Based on some estimates, guns are statistically like rats. They outnumber our population. Not surprisingly, our output of ammunition for civilian firearms almost staggers the imagination. American industry outdoes all other nations in the production of bullets. Nearly five billion rounds of ammunition flow through the marketplace each year. That is enough, laid end to end, to stretch a bandoleer of ammunition three times around the equator. All of those bullets could not only wipe out the world's entire human population but destroy much of the world's wildlife as well.

FEBRUARY 17, 1971

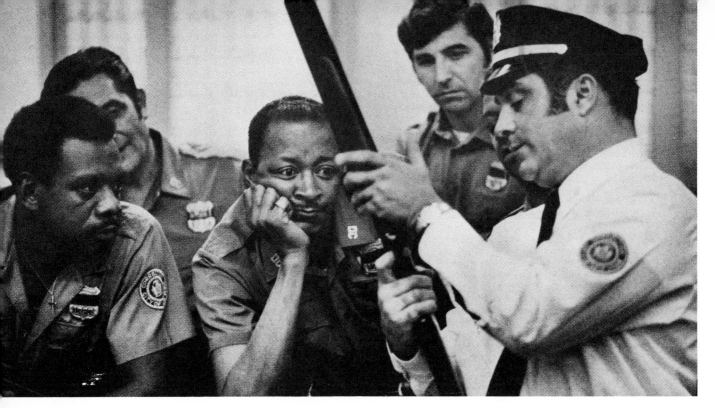

There is solid evidence that gun control can bring the crime rate down. The most dramatic immediate reduction would be in the number of killings which occur during family quarrels and neighborhood fights. If a gun is not on a closet shelf or in a table drawer, an angry domestic argument is unlikely to escalate into a corpse on the family floor.

Many members of the Senate and the House are already convinced that gun control is necessary. But legislation has been slow to come. Like other aggressive minorities in politics, the gun lobby gets its way by following up its opinions with action on election day.

To win on gun control in Congress, it is necessary for citizens to build a countervailing force. We can end the power of the gun lobby in American politics. All that Washington is waiting for is a sign that the people really care about the issue.

OCTOBER 21, 1976

I see America now, moving beyond the Age of the Soldier and entering the Age of Justice, an age of challenge and opportunity that can be the most satisfying and rewarding and productive of all the ages of our nation. The question for our generation and our children's generation is, How long can America make its Age of Justice last?

AUGUST 12, 1977

YOUNG AND OLD

Those who died at Kent State did not perish in battle or at the barricades. They did not run the heroes' hazard or seek the glory of martyrdom. They were young and free and American. And so, in the year of our Lord 1970, they died; and at the hands of their countrymen. These young people, in the manner of their dying, have opened a gap in nature itself, through which, for a moment, we can see ourselves and reflect. It has stripped away the fragile cover of hypocrisy and reassurance from the turbulent unrest of American life. It has illuminated the corruption of obsolete dogmas. It tells us that power which is arrogant or indifferent is at war with the liberation of the human spirit; that power unrestrained by moral values of the people—as they themselves see those needs—must either perish or maintain itself by force.

MAY 8, 1970

We are not educating because it will improve the material well-being of our country, although it will do that. We are not educating because it will lead to technical progress, although it will do that as well. We are educating for the future of our democracy, so that young men and women can prepare for their roles as citizens in society—as participants in the great constitutional experiment of self-government that our ancestors began two hundred years ago.

OCTOBER 25, 1978

If there are some children in this land—whether because they are black or because they were born on a reservation or because they speak a different language or because they are poor—if there are some children who do not have an equal opportunity for a quality education, then there are some children who are not free.

APRIL 25, 1977

One special area of deep concern to me is the inaccessibility of education in this rich but negligent and wasteful nation of ours.

Perhaps you can go to the local bank for a loan, or to the government for a scholarship. But only one student in five gets a loan or scholarship. And those loans and scholarships do not cover the full cost of college. Next, you try to find a part-time job, or ask your parents to pay the difference, so you can get a college education. Worst of all, if these methods fail, you decide that you can't enroll in the college of your choice, or perhaps in any college at all.

No young American should be put in that position. This is a bountiful country and a challenging country, but the bounty and challenge depend upon people educated to do the jobs that must be done.

OCTOBER 25, 1978

If I can leave a single message with the younger generation, it is to lash yourself to the mast, like Ulysses if you must, to escape the siren calls of complacency and indifference.

JUNE 4, 1978

You did not make the world you live in, but you have the chance to change it, to leave it better than you found it.

JUNE 19, 1977

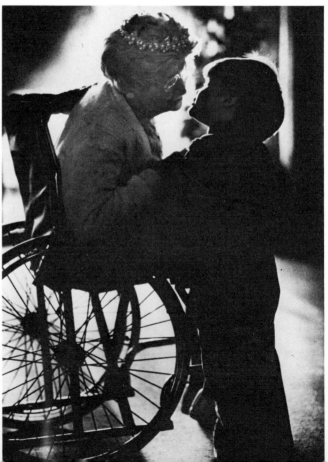

The time has come to lower the voting age to eighteen in the United States, and thereby bring our youth into the mainstream of the political process. I believe this is the most important single principle we can pursue as a nation if we are to succeed in bringing our youth into full and lasting participation in our institutions of democratic government.

FEBRUARY 23, 1970

Too often, preoccupied with busy lives and careers and interests, parents are willing now to let other institutions take over the job of raising children. The school and the church are, and ought to be, vital shaping influences on young men and women in every community. But they are not surrogates for homes and parents. When parents neglect this primary responsibility, no other institution can fill the gap.

MAY 26, 1976

It is the young who have often been the first to speak and act against injustice or corruption or tyranny, wherever it is found. More than any other group in the population, it is the young who refuse to allow a difficulty or a challenge to become an excuse to fail to meet it. We need the ideas and ideals, the spirit and dedication of young Americans who are willing to hold a mirror to society and probe the sores that others would ignore.

FEBRUARY 9, 1976

One of the finest chapters in the history of America's long and tragic involvement in Vietnam was written by the millions of young men and women who first saw the truth about the war and persuaded America to turn back. One of the finest chapters in the recent history of civil rights was written by the youth of America and the freedom riders of the early 1960s. One of the finest chapters in America's concern for the impoverished people of the world was written by young persons in the Peace Corps overseas and in our domestic service programs here at home.

OCTOBER 1, 1976

You don't have to be a senator to make things change. You don't have to make a headline. In our country today and in nations throughout the world, young Americans are doing many worthwhile things.

Young physicians are bringing health care to people and places that never had a doctor. Young teachers are bringing knowledge and opportunity to children who never had a school. Young lawyers are bringing the Constitution to people who never knew the Bill of Rights. Young business men and women are bringing new enterprises to the city ghetto and the rural farm, and helping to end the ancient curse of poverty and neglect. In many parts of America and the world, young Americans are making a real and very important difference for their fellow human beings.

OCTOBER 1, 1976

To those who hesitate to begin the journey because the road appears too difficult or success too distant, I reply that not within my lifetime have I seen such extraordinary opportunities for change and progress on so many fronts as I see today. The strenuous efforts of those who went before us have opened many doors. The torch of leadership is passing to a new generation. All you have to do is pick it up and help to guide the way.

You will see many wrongs and evils and injustices on your journey. These flaws in our society and in the world have been caused by human beings, and therefore they can be resolved by human beings.

I urge you to nourish these qualities—timeless virtues like courage and compassion, justice and integrity, involvement and concern. These qualities are tools that will not fail. They are waiting for your use, and you will find they are more powerful than any weapon of oppression or resistance.

JUNE 19, 1977

I can think of no group that deserves more attention from its elected representatives than the nation's elderly. They have built the factories and mills of America. They have fought in our defense. They have paid the taxes to finance the growth of our cities and towns. And they have worked and struggled and sacrificed for a lifetime to see that our children will have a better chance to realize their dreams.

MARCH 25, 1975

They represent one of the most wasted human resources in this country. No truly great nation can afford to waste the experience and wisdom accumulated over a lifetime. Because one reaches a particular age—whether thirty or sixty-five—does not mean there are limitations on the ability to learn, the ability to think, or the ability to contribute to our community and our country.

JUNE 25, 1976

Society fails to recognize the potential of the elderly and the vast reservoir of talent, skill, and experience they offer to the country. Frank Lloyd Wright was seventy-six when he designed the Guggenheim Museum. Albert Schweitzer was seventy-eight when he won the Nobel Peace Prize. At sixty-nine, Benjamin Franklin helped to draft the Declaration of Independence; from seventy to seventy-nine, he served as ambassador to France; and at eighty-one, he participated actively in the Constitutional Convention that launched the nation. Oliver Wendell Holmes, second only perhaps to John Marshall among the giants of American jurisprudence, was appointed to the Supreme Court at the age of sixty-one and served brilliantly until he retired at ninety.

APRIL 23, 1976

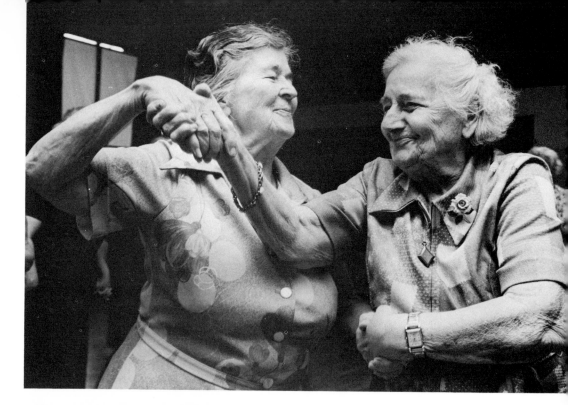

Too many elderly Americans are standing in unemployment lines. Too many elderly men and women are unable to afford the fuel they need to heat their homes. Too many older Americans are forced to skimp on the food they eat and on the clothes they wear.

JUNE 13, 1975

Let us understand the debt that we owe to those who have built this country for us, and begin to make good on it.

FEBRUARY 1, 1978

Old age should not be a time of silence, a time of isolation, a time of inactivity. We have the resources to insure that the heritage of old age is one of dignity, not despair. We have the resources and we have the capacity. Let us show that we also have the wisdom.

How we meet the challenges facing the nation's elderly will determine the quality of life and of social justice for all Americans in our third century.

OCTOBER 2, 1975

A BASIC RIGHT TO HEALTH FOR ALL

One of the saddest ironies in the worldwide movement for social justice in the twentieth century is that America now stands virtually alone in the international community on national health insurance. It seems that every nation is out of step but Uncle Sam. With the sole exception of South Africa, no other industrial nation in the world leaves its citizens in fear of financial ruin because of illness.

DECEMBER 9, 1978

Why can England, Israel, Denmark, and Sweden protect their people against financial barriers to health care, when America cannot? How can these European countries afford to make health care a basic right for their people, when the wealthiest nation in the world cannot?

Why can Norway, Sweden, and Finland provide district health officers for Lapland, when we can't find doctors to serve the poor of Appalachia or the migrants on the western slopes of the Rockies?

Why can the State of Israel place doctors in a family-health-care center to treat Arabs in the desert, when the ghettos of every major city in America cry out for medical attention?

OCTOBER 1, 1971

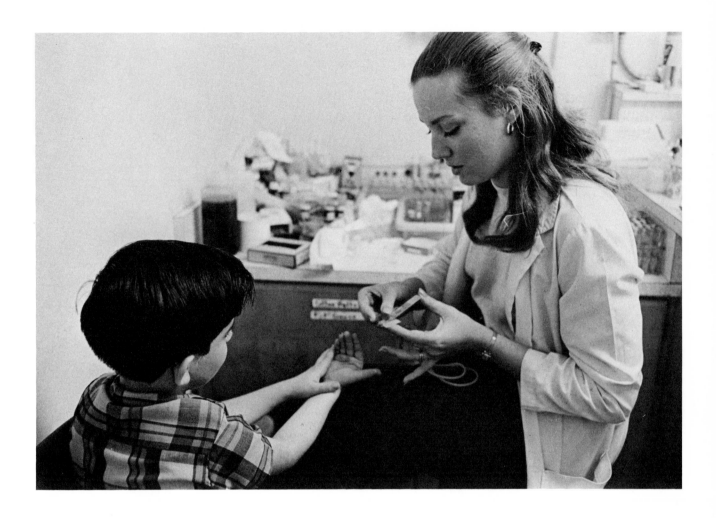

If infant mortality were as low in America as it is in Sweden, fifty thousand fewer American babies would have died last year. That's the sum total of all the American soldiers killed in the entire Vietnam War, and it happened in America in 1970.

APRIL 12, 1971

Today's hearing is about the erosion of the people's trust and faith in their government. For the record will show that for over twenty years the federal government placed the citizens of Utah at risk without their consent, without their knowledge and without taking proper precautions. The record will show that the nuclear-weapons tests conducted in the 1950s may very well have resulted in the cancers of the 1960s and 1970s. The record will show that the people of Utah, who have always prided themselves on their patriotism, and who believed the repeated assurances of their government, have come to feel they were misled, perhaps even deceived, by that government.

APRIL 19, 1979

83

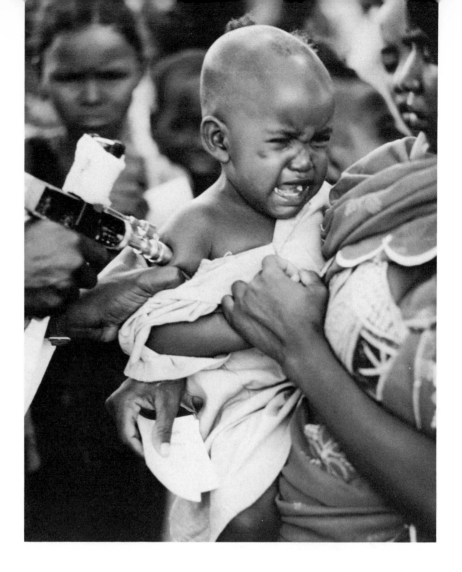

In many poverty-stricken corners of the world, death is never far from the baby's crib. In one nation in Latin America, eighty percent of all deaths are accounted for by children under five years of age. In the developing nations as a whole, young children account for half of all the deaths. How many parents in Europe know that? How many parents in the United States know that children in Latin America are dying in vast numbers because of malnutrition? How many of us realize that the visit these children most often pay is to the mortician, not the pediatrician?

Behind the figures are the people, the hundreds of millions of human beings living lives of desperation. Fear and hunger, sickness and death are the horsemen of their daily living apocalypse.

How do we deal with a drug that may be ruled unsafe in America because it causes cancer in later life, but that may mean the difference between survival and death for a child in another land?

A world that is spending $300 billion a year for arms can spend a little more for health. And it may well be that what we do in health will be as important to world peace and cooperation in the long run as what we achieve in arms control, and at a tiny fraction of the cost.

MAY 6, 1977

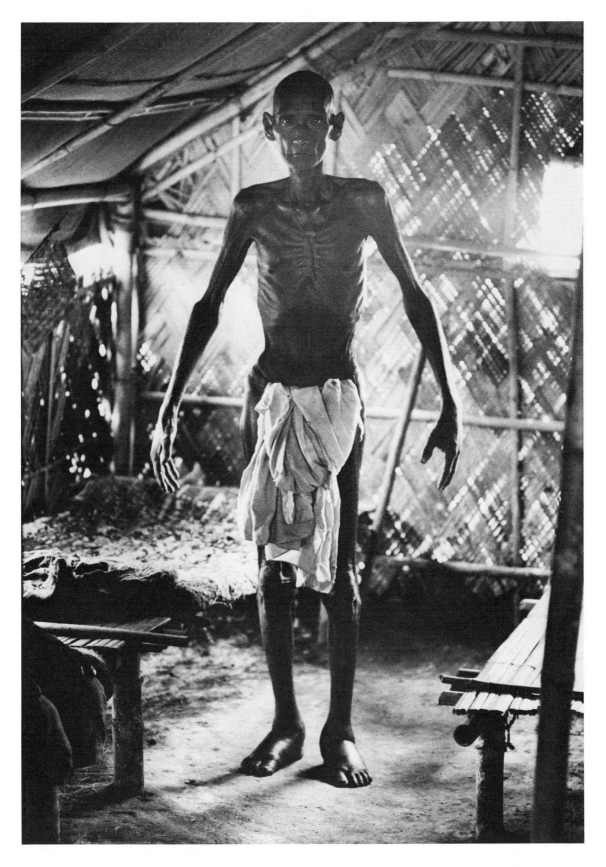

I have walked through the refugee camps in Bangladesh and the Middle East. I have seen lifetimes of hunger packed into lives of children too young to understand their condition. I have seen their small figures, warped and deformed from malnutrition. I have seen their parents, aged before their time, hollowed eyes peering out of bodies wracked with disease. Let me cite a few examples that are vividly in my mind:

I have seen children suffering from schistosomiasis, bellies swollen with the hard and ugly tumors caused by infestations of the worm.

A seven-year-old boy in Dacca was weak and dehydrated from disease brought on by malnutrition and his vulnerability to infection.

A woman tended by her husband was suffering from tetanus. She was being treated in a hospital in Bangladesh—one of the few lucky enough to reach a hospital in time.

A red-haired, bright-eyed girl in eastern India had swollen limbs from kwashiorkor, caused by famine and malnutrition.

A young boy had a face forever scarred by smallpox.

A Bengali mother held her two children, one aged fourteen months and the other seven years. But there was no difference in their size.

Young children, seemingly healthy, squinted in the sunlight, a sign of early degeneration of their eyes through vitamin insufficiency.

For most of us, the worldwide pain, debility, and misery inflicted by preventable illness cannot be understood by facts and figures alone. You have to see the victims yourself, to understand the horror of their plight and to realize the enormous waste in human life that is taking place today in many lands.

MAY 6, 1977

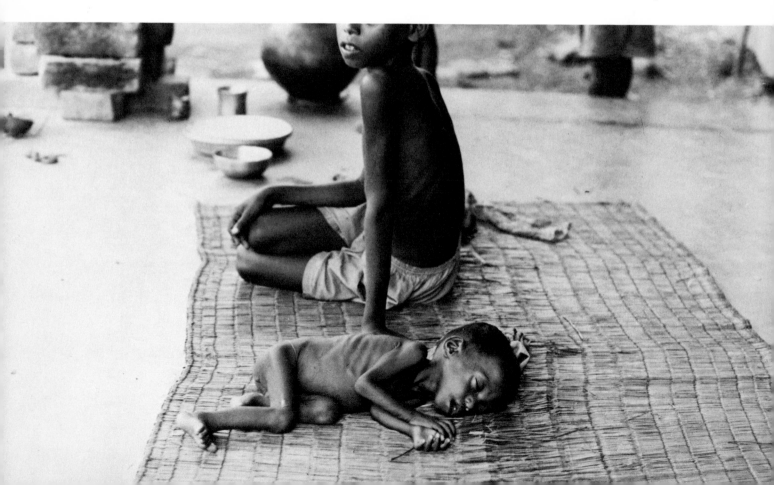

In Canada, across the border, they have a system that gives decent care with tough controls on costs. It isn't socialized medicine, and it doesn't put a government bureaucrat beside the doctor at the bedside of the patient. The Canadian experience proves that a common-sense approach can solve the complex modern crisis over health, and it's time America solved its crisis, too.

OCTOBER 23, 1978

America leads the world in Nobel Prizes for medical research, but we are winning no prizes for our ability to bring the laboratory to the bedside of the patient.

MAY 17, 1975

One of the most distressing things about modern America is that in our unbelievably rich land the quality of health care available to large numbers of our people is unbelievably poor.

OCTOBER 15, 1975

America doesn't need a double standard of health —one for those who can afford it and another for those who can't.

FEBRUARY 1, 1976

If we deny the finest health care to any citizens, we deny the value of their lives. They become slaves of unnecessary suffering and disability. The promise of a bountiful society acquires a hollow ring. The American dream becomes a nightmare.

OCTOBER 5, 1975

The health-care crisis has many faces.

It is a union brewer from Queens, whose kidney dialysis machine is about to be unplugged unless he can pay $10,000 a year for its cost.

It is a ghetto mother in the Bronx, whose oldest son is severely retarded for life because of lead paint poisoning, but whose younger children have not yet even been tested for symptoms of the disease.

It is a Cornell engineering student, paralyzed for life by a tragic football injury, whose upper-middle-class family has been ruined by the devastating financial consequences of the accident—$50,000 in five months, and no end in sight. The family thought they were protected, because the father was an insurance salesman who carried the best health policy his company offered.

It is an elderly widow in West Virginia whose husband died of black-lung disease, and who now lives on a benefit of eighty-four dollars a month. She pays five dollars a month for insurance to cover the Medicare deductibles and coinsurance. Her doctor refuses to fill out any of the insurance forms, so she has to do it all herself.

It is a paint sprayer for a bridge company in Nashville, who lost his health insurance when his company went out of business. He had to file for bankruptcy because he couldn't pay a $600 hospital bill when his son was born.

It is a disabled World War II veteran living on a pension of two hundred dollars a month, and paying four dollars a month on what he still owes from a 1968 hospital bill.

It is a black father in Chicago, who told us how his ten-year-old son died at the emergency-room door while St. George's Hospital checked the family's financial condition to see if they could pay the bill.

It is a college linguistics professor dead of brain cancer at forty-six after tens of thousands of dollars in expenses. Now the lives of his wife and children are mortgaged for years into the future. The cruelest irony is that the wife is from Israel, where all of her expenses would be covered.

It is countless citizens harassed by bill collectors hired by hospitals that are better at chasing patients than at treating them.

We have learned that a $500 expense for a working man or woman can be just as catastrophic as a $50,000 expense for a business executive. We have learned that even the cost of health-insurance premiums and Medicare deductibles can be catastrophic expenses for millions of senior citizens.

APRIL 26, 1971

88

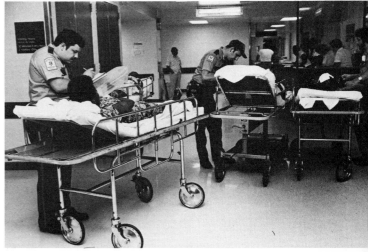

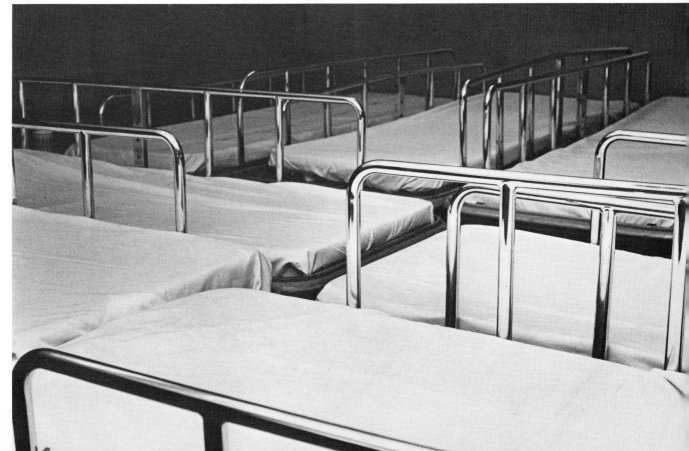

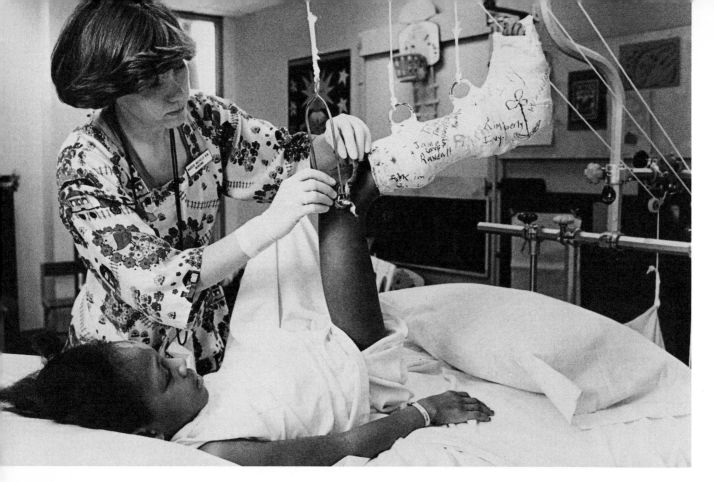

There are those who say it is un-American for the government to intervene in the way we do business in the health-care industry. This is utter nonsense.

If anything, the health-care industry is itself un-American in the way it does business. In America we rely on competition and the informed choice of individual citizens to guarantee that products are available at reasonable prices in the marketplace. But where do we see doctors or hospitals actually competing in the American health-care industry? Where do we find consumers able to judge quality well enough to compare the health services they receive?

Things simply don't operate this way in the medical marketplace. Doctors reach tacit agreements about prices among themselves, with the active support and blessing of the insurance industry. They refer their patients to hospitals, which charge what they please and then coerce the insurance industry into paying whatever price they think the public will bear.

Surely, we cannot rely on competition and consumer choice to keep the health-care industry innovative and responsive to the country's needs.

APRIL 26, 1971

Health care has become so expensive that Americans are now working more than one full month of every year just to pay for their health care—two weeks' wages for hospital care alone.

JUNE 17, 1977

90

We have reached a turning point in America's health care—the point where rising costs threaten to force us either to retreat from the social progress we've already made or to take bold action to reform our health care system under a program of national health insurance. If we don't do something soon to reform our health-care system, no one will be able to afford good health care—not the federal government, not the states, and not the average American family.

JUNE 24, 1975

We can no longer continue to squander billions of dollars on unnecessary drugs, hospitalization, surgery, and technology while hundreds of thousands of children are not being immunized and millions of needy Americans can't get basic care.

JUNE 17, 1977

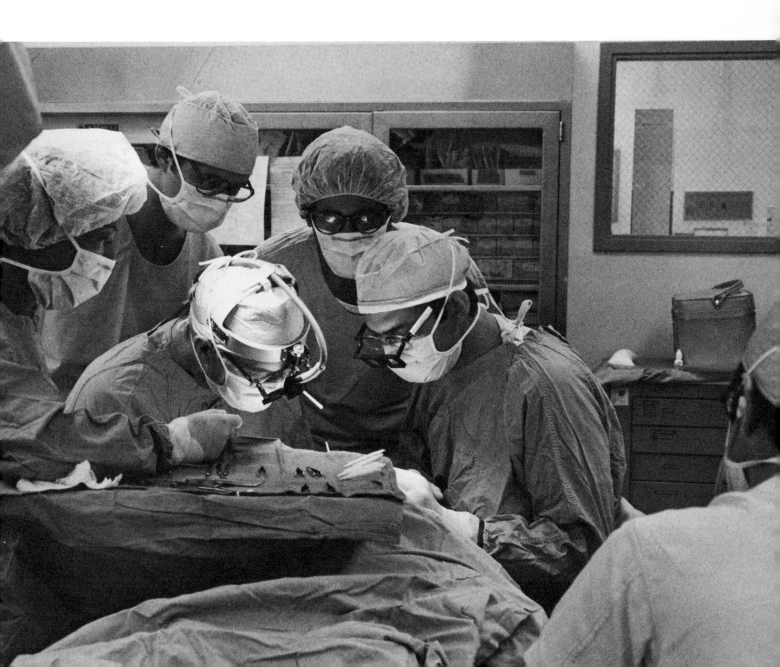

The doctors and the hospitals are not the villains. They, like us, are the victims, caught in a system that contains the wrong incentives and that rewards the worst inefficiencies. If we are to succeed in our goal of achieving health reform, we must break the trap that binds us and free the hospitals and the doctors to create a health-care system worthy of this nation.

APRIL 26, 1971

We are learning that the world in which we have lived comfortably for many years is fraught with potential dangers. For many long-accepted benefits, there are prices to be paid and risks to be taken. The food we eat, the water we drink, the air we breathe, the chemicals we use, the energy we rely on, all may, at various times, present serious public-health problems.

Look what the average family with school-age children has been told in recent years: the bacon on the breakfast table, the saccharin in the diet soda, the asbestos in the school walls, the hair dryer in the home, the steak on the charcoal grill, the ingredients in over-the-counter drugs—all these parts of our daily lives may cause cancer. If this family lives in a city, they may suffer through pollution alerts with unhealthy air, and their water supply may have dangerously high chemical levels. If they live near a coal mine or a chemical dump or a nuclear power plant, they face other hazards.

MAY 31, 1979

Current regulatory policy is a maze of contradictions. We allow cigarettes on the market, knowing that they cause thousands of deaths and hundreds of thousands of illnesses, but we ban Tris and red dye number 2. We place limits on advertising of cigarettes and spend public dollars on antismoking campaigns, but spend a great deal more public money subsidizing the tobacco industry. We require seat belts in cars, but do not require that they be worn or that cars be limited to safer speeds. We allow carcinogens to abound in our air and water but not our food supply. We require that drugs be proven safe and effective for a given purpose before marketing, but allow physicians to use them for any purpose and in any dosage once they are on the market. We allow risk/benefit criteria to be applied to drugs and medical devices but not to food additives. We send conflicting messages to the American people and thus undermine the credibility of our regulatory effort. As a result, they stop taking our warnings seriously.

OCTOBER 31, 1977

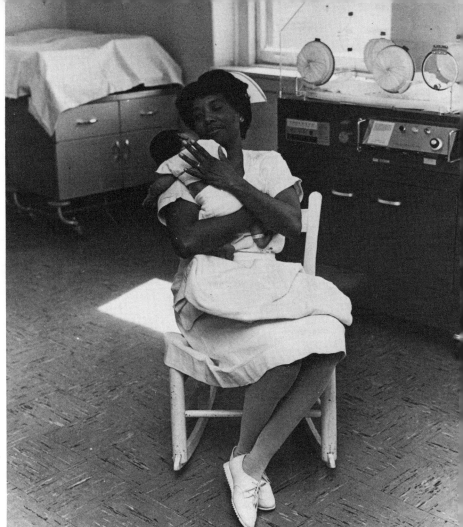

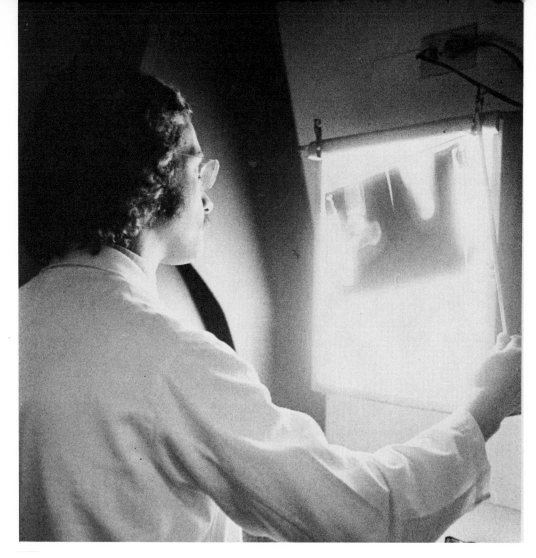

Eight million Americans—largely workers and their families—have been exposed to asbestos since World War II, of whom 200,000 may die of lung cancer. This is a national tragedy of staggering proportions. And it will be repeated with other substances unless we vigorously enforce existing laws protecting the work place and our environment against toxic hazards.

JULY 25, 1978

We are only now beginning to understand the health implications of exposure to low-level radiation. We are only now learning that the risk is cumulative, increasing over time—long periods of time. We are only now learning to correlate the medical occurrences of today with environmental exposures that took place, or began, decades before.

APRIL 19, 1979

94

One of the most far-reaching efforts in improving our health-care system has been our commitment to preventive health care and health-maintenance organizations. Few actions will be more important for the long-run good health of the American people than the steps we are taking now to emphasize prevention of disease as a key element of our health care system.

An ounce of prevention may be worth a pound of cure in many different areas of life. But in terms of health-care dollars, it is fair to say that millions for prevention may save us billions that we would otherwise have to spend to pay the cost of treatment.

APRIL 9, 1978

What we have today in the United States is not so much a health-care system as a disease-cure system.

MAY 31, 1979

Just over a century ago, well before we knew of bacteria or viruses, pioneers in public health began the conquest of the infectious diseases. They used simple methods—sanitation, improved hygiene, improved nutrition—but the results were almost incredible. They made major inroads against tuberculosis, typhus, diphtheria, scarlet fever, cholera, tetanus, and other communicable conditions which were then the greatest scourges of humanity. Between 1900 and 1950, life expectancy in this country increased from 47.3 years to 68.2 years. That was an achievement unparalleled in history. It was made possible by a positive health strategy—one that emphasized the maintenance of good health and the prevention of disease.

The time has come to formulate another positive health strategy for the United States, by concentrating more attention and resources on the prevention of disease. I am committed to disease prevention, not just because it is good fiscal strategy, but because it is good health strategy; not just because it will save money, but because it will save lives; not just because it will increase worker productivity, but because it will improve the quality of our existence on this planet.

JULY 25, 1978

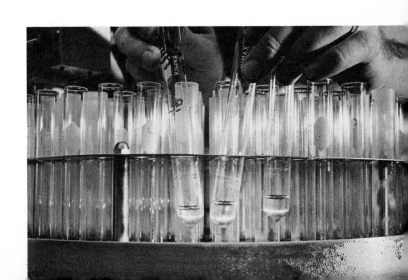

Medicare was delayed for a decade and more, while the country argued about socialized medicine and ignored the health of its senior citizens.

NOVEMBER 2, 1975

You will hear it said that the fight is about socialized medicine, or about government intrusion into the relationship between physician and patient, or about preserving the role of private enterprise in the health-insurance field. This is not what the debate on health care is all about. At bottom, the debate is about a very simple principle—whether decent health care is to be a basic right for all the people of this land.

APRIL 11, 1975

Children should not grow up in America with twisted limbs or retarded minds, simply because their parents cannot afford the care they need. Families should not be dumped into poverty by unnecessary illness and disability. No American should face financial disaster because of the costs of decent health. No American should give up his children's education, or exhaust his savings, or mortgage his home and future, to pay the cost of health.

OCTOBER 15, 1975

A comprehensive universal system of national health insurance is required in order to realize that right for all Americans. Quality health care in America requires a concerted effort at disease prevention, at health-care planning, at maintaining a vigorous biomedical research effort, at assuring equity of access to medical services, at developing a national manpower policy and at establishing quality controls.

What we need is universal coverage of all Americans under the same health-care program, regardless of income, place of work, age, past medical history, sex, race, or any other factor. The program must offer comprehensive benefits, including care in the doctor's office as well as the hospital. And it must also emphasize preventive care, early diagnosis, and treatment.

OCTOBER 31, 1977

Our witnesses from Detroit live just a few miles from our witnesses across the border in Canada. Mr. Kovaks of Detroit and Mr. Norris of Windsor, Canada, are both retired auto workers.

96

Mr. Kovaks' wife has suffered irreversible brain damage and requires nursing-home care. Mr. Kovaks has had to exhaust his savings to pay $20,000 for his wife's medical bills before becoming eligible for Medicaid.

Mr. Norris also has required extensive hospitalization since his retirement. His tremendous medical bills have been covered by Canada's national health insurance. He does not have to worry about his health-insurance benefits running out after retirement, or when he isn't working. He does not have to qualify for Medicaid.

What a difference there is between the Kovaks and Norris families. Their stories make a compelling case for national health insurance in America.

OCTOBER 23, 1978

We have expanded our alcoholism and drug treatment programs, yet have failed abysmally to develop effective programs to understand and treat these afflictions.

We have had exposé after exposé on the problems of child abuse, and yet the problem remains poorly understood and out of control.

We have identified the special emotional problems of children and adolescents exacerbated by the rapidly changing nature of American society, but have failed to develop effective treatments or even to make existing services accessible.

FEBRUARY 7, 1979

97

Mental illness—poorly understood by scientists, inadequately treated by physicians, feared by most Americans—continues to cause more individual and family suffering than any other condition in American life. Today, at any given moment, as much as ten to fifteen percent of the entire population of the United States needs some form of mental-health service. Yet for millions of Americans—the very young and the very old, the urban poor and the migrant farmworker, the physically handicapped and the Vietnam veteran, the black and Hispanic American, and people of every age with chronic mental illness—the needed services are lacking.

And although we have publicly discussed mental illness, we have failed to remove the stigma attached to it—a stigma which reflects an irrational fear of an American "Heart of Darkness."

FEBRUARY 7, 1979

In the rapid pace of society and its emphasis on youth and mobility, the handicapped have been left behind, relegated to the backwaters of society, ostracized by their contemporaries, victimized by unfair attitudes of discrimination.

JUNE 28, 1978

Only a decade or two ago, the concept of equal rights for the retarded would not have been taken seriously. The tragedy for the nation is that millions of human beings capable of contributing to society, capable of achieving something that they could be proud of, and capable of individual happiness, were shut away forever.

OCTOBER 12, 1976

A basic question is whether our law, in its present form, can guarantee the civil and legal rights of retarded persons in the community. I have long felt that we must find ways to protect the rights of those who cannot protect themselves or advance their own interest, and in a way which assures them the full personal freedom to make the decisions they can. We must take steps to assure that each mentally retarded citizen will lead a fulfilling life, a life of dignity and self-respect, a life in which each will achieve the maximum of his or her potential.

OCTOBER 27, 1976

We must secure an era of full justice for the retarded citizens of our society.

OCTOBER 12, 1976

Society is often fearful of those who are different. And so progress is slow in breaking down the walls of prejudice and the barriers of indifference. The recognition of the rights of the retarded has come grudgingly and unwillingly. But it is under way. The doors and windows of our institutions have slowly begun to open. The light is coming in.

OCTOBER 25, 1975

A SOUND ECONOMY

A sound economy is the greatest social program America ever had, the source of our hopes for action on all the other issues facing us. This is our most important goal, to bring our sick economy back to health.

APRIL 2, 1976

A weak American economy poses the greatest threat today to international economic stability.

So long as the economy is wrong, nothing else is right.

JANUARY 21, 1977

The first American revolution began when the colonists took up arms at Concord Bridge. In a few short years, another revolution also began in Massachusetts, the Industrial Revolution that made our nation possible.

Immigrant Irish laborers walked from Boston to Lowell to begin construction of the canals and the mills. As if touched by a magic wand, there sprang up the long red mills, the boardinghouses for the working men and women, the amazing locks and canals, the churning water wheels that tamed the running power of the river, the incredible machinery that transformed thin strands of cotton thread into cloth and clothing for the expanding American nation.

MARCH 1, 1976

The history of this nation rests on the skills of its workers no less than it does on the achievements of its scholars.

It is a history of workers who pulled steel bars from Pennsylvania furnaces to gird our skyscrapers.

It is a history of fishermen who set out from Cape Cod in the cold hours before dawn to help feed a nation.

It is a history of men and women whose talents, ingenuity, and determination comprise our most valuable natural resource.

OCTOBER 19, 1975

101

A fifty-nine-year-old engineer from Lincoln, Massachusetts, testified that he had been out of work for sixteen months. After fourteen years with his last employer, he received four days' notice before separation. But although the human being was discarded, his ideas remained the property of the firm. The company has since received patents on two applications he had pending before his dismissal.

A communications engineer from Cherry Hill, New Jersey, led the team which designed the antenna for the Lunar Rover vehicle on Apollo 15. This antenna permitted the astronauts to transmit their findings as they explored the surface of the moon. The design was so successful that the engineer received a special commendation from NASA for his leadership. He also received a layoff notice from his firm shortly before he watched his antenna in action on the surface of the moon.

A fifty-nine-year-old aeronautical engineer from Seattle, unemployed for thirteen months, told how earlier in his career he had turned down an opportunity for a tenured professorship at a leading university because he did not want to give up his work on government-sponsored aerospace programs.

These are not people who have lost their jobs through any fault of their own. They are highly competent individuals who have performed successfully over the years, and have now been placed on the shelf because of shifting national programs far beyond their control.

NOVEMBER 3, 1971

I have known and talked with fishermen from the great ports at New Bedford, Gloucester, and Boston all my life. I have known their courage, their strength, their humor, their traditions and folklore, and their pride in lives spent at sea.

But now, speaking with these same men I hear of frustration; of fear; of despair; of a ghost that once was the pride of all New England and all the nation.

MARCH 30, 1971

The fishing industry is Massachusetts' and America's oldest industry. Many of our most picturesque and attractive coastal towns and cities grew because the fishing industry was a vital part of the growing national economy. There are few families in Massachusetts that do not share in the heritage of the fishing industry in one way or another. And there are none of us in Massachusetts who do not understand our very special relationship with the sea.

If the tradition of independence and courage and hard work that gave birth to this nation is strong anywhere, it is in the fishing industry. If there is a more exciting and vigorous career for young people than in a revitalized fishing industry, I have not heard it.

OCTOBER 29, 1976

103

It is one of the great tragedies of life when a healthy person who wants to work cannot find a job and cannot support a family. Unemployment can strip a person of dignity, self-respect, and hope. It can make a person lose faith in the future.

OCTOBER 19, 1975

There are some who even now are prepared to declare victory in the war against unemployment. They want to turn to a single-minded war against inflation. They say that the national unemployment rate has been falling steadily for many months. But as long as unemployment of black teenagers in Harlem and South Philadelphia and Watts and Roxbury is still at forty percent or worse—as long as half of those young Americans are not even counted in the labor force—they have no right to claim victory against unemployment. Even as we fight harder against inflation, we cannot abandon the unemployed.

MAY 7, 1978

Inflation is a serious problem. Its solution is going to strain our most enlightened economists and policy-makers. But let us get on with the job of finding the right remedies for inflation, without resorting to the time-dishonored tactic of ravaging the economy in the process. If we learn anything from our present troubles, let it be the lesson that this is the last time the nation will have to suffer because of the dangerous myth that a scorched-earth policy of recession is the answer to inflation.

MARCH 12, 1975

This nation cannot allow its economy to drift toward the future as though ten or fifteen percent inflation were the natural order of the American economic universe.

JUNE 14, 1979

One of the basic assumptions of our political system is that large centers of unaccountable power are inconsistent with democratic government and the values of a free society. If there is a single theme that ties together the best in both liberal and conservative political traditions, it is this hostility to unchecked power. If the awesome power of giant corporations is no longer adequately checked by the discipline of the market, it is not just our pocketbook that is in jeopardy, it is our liberty.

MAY 3, 1977

Except in matters of health and safety, our society has wisely chosen the competition of private unregulated business as the best way to ensure that consumers are offered the products and services they desire at prices they can afford.

APRIL 19, 1978

For too long, we have accepted a watchmaker's theory of the federal universe. Congress and the Administration construct the programs and set them ticking—and then leave them running on their own for years or even decades.

APRIL 29, 1976

Our lives and our economy are increasingly caught up in an ever-constricting web of laws and regulations that threaten to bring our vaunted free enterprise system to its knees unless we act.

The fall of the Ottoman Empire at the beginning of this century is widely attributed to the excesses of a top-heavy civil service and a system of administrative regulation imposed by a bureaucracy run wild.

The traditional American reaction to a problem or abuse has been to say, "There ought to be a law." But now, as we survey the complex legal framework of the nation, we should also be prepared to say of many areas, "There ought *not* to be a law."

JUNE 14, 1979

Agencies of the federal government have destroyed competition in one of the remaining free marketplaces of air transportation. They have also virtually guaranteed that the student, the senior citizen, the laborer, the farmhand, the small businessman—average Americans for whom air charter travel represents the difference between staying home and seeing the world—will be paying higher prices

for that once-in-a-lifetime trip to Europe. That is, if they can now afford to make the trip in the first place.

Restrictive regulatory policies and closed procedures may mean not only higher prices and poorer service to the consumer; they can at the same time portend injury to the airlines as well.

NOVEMBER 7, 1974

The airline deregulation bill is the most important piece of regulatory reform legislation ever produced by Congress. The benefits of deregulation are already being felt by both the industry and consumers. Never before have fares been lower, planes fuller and airline profits higher.

OCTOBER 6, 1978

It was such a simple idea. For America, it was like reinventing the wheel. We rediscovered competition. The elaborate scheme of federal airline regulation turned out to be a house of cards. It wasn't working, and at last we were wise enough to tear it down. There have been few more satisfying achievements in Congress in recent years than the success of airline deregulation. It has been good for the industry, good for the consumer, and good for the economy.

JUNE 14, 1979

It is time to substantially reduce ICC regulation of the trucking industry and eliminate the industry's antitrust immunity for price fixing.

Federal regulation of trucking was imposed more than forty years ago, when the trucking industry was in its infancy and when the nation was in the middle of its most serious depression—and when, largely as a result of that depression, distrust of private enterprise and unregulated competition was high.

The trucking industry is no longer in its infancy. It is now a $108-billion-a-year business. It accounts for more than 75 percent of the total revenues earned by all forms of transportation. It is a mature, prosperous and inherently competitive industry. It no longer needs the extensive economic protection of a bygone age.

The distinction between shipments which are regulated and those which are not makes no sense.

It makes no sense to regulate shipments of roasted or boiled nuts but not shipments of raw nuts, shelled or unshelled.

It makes no sense to regulate shipments of wheat germ but not of whole wheat.

It makes no sense to regulate shipments of racehorses, but not of riding horses for pleasure.

It makes no sense to regulate shipments of beef that is dressed and frozen but not of poultry that is dressed and frozen.

It makes no sense to regulate cut vegetables depending on how long they are steamed and at what temperature before shipping.

It makes no sense to regulate frozen TV dinners if they are beef, spaghetti, or veal but not if they are chicken or seafood.

It makes no sense to regulate shipments of raisins if they are coated with chocolate but not if they are coated with honey.

These distinctions reveal the absurdity of trying to regulate half an industry, when the other half operates more efficiently free from regulation. Our fundamental national interest in a more productive, fuel-efficient, and responsive transportation system can best be achieved with less regulation and more reliance on private initiative.

JUNE 26, 1979

The trucking industry maintains that without regulation, small communities would lose service. None of the evidence supports this view. A 1977 study showed that small communities are served not because of regulation by the Interstate Commerce Commission, but because business is good and truckers want to serve them. Moreover, truckers who haul unprocessed agricultural products are all unregulated, yet they serve every small community in America. The ICC doesn't force them to do so. In fact, the ICC doesn't force anyone to provide a service they don't want to. The idea that regulation is what ensures service is a myth that should be laid firmly to rest.

MAY 17, 1979

Investigations of three federal agencies—the Civil Aeronautics Board, the Food and Drug Administration, and the Federal Energy Administration—suggest that different answers will be required for different agencies.

Sometimes we need less regulation, as in the case of naturally competitive industries like the airlines.

Sometimes we need more but better regulation, as in the case of the pharmaceutical industry and other areas where the public health and safety are involved.

Sometimes we need regulation that is capable of dealing quickly with a shortage or other sudden emergency, as in the case of the Arab oil embargo.

Sometimes we need "split-level" regulation, capable of recognizing that what is fair for General Motors is not necessarily fair for small business.

APRIL 29, 1976

The reservoir of goodwill toward small business that exists in Congress demands an end to the second-class status to which small business has been relegated for so long. The problem of overregulation has been a source of growing friction between government and business in many areas. But nowhere is the problem more acute than in the regulations that affect small business.

Procrustes was the villain in ancient mythology who seized his victims and made them fit his iron bed, either by stretching them if they were too short or by cutting off their limbs if they were too long.

Too often, the same practice is followed by federal agencies, making small business fit frameworks of economic regulation designed for other enterprises.

APRIL 29, 1976

Frequently in the past, small business has played the role of poor cousin whenever the interests of business are considered by government at any level —federal, state, or local.

MAY 26, 1978

Among the innovative or high-technology companies in the U.S., there is mounting evidence that smaller firms far surpass larger firms in the rate of innovation and job creation.

MAY 3, 1979

Small business has played a prominent role in our national economy throughout the two hundred years of our history, and it continues to play a prominent role today. Half our population—100 million Americans—depend for their livelihood on small business. Half our gross national product and half our total business employment in the United States are provided by small business.

APRIL 29, 1976

Many Americans do not understand the role of competition in today's complex and increasingly confusing marketplace. I regard competition as the cornerstone of our free-enterprise system. Along with the Bill of Rights, it is the most important distinguishing feature of our nation in the world community, a beacon for many other nations who are striving to emulate our two-hundred-year-old example of freedom and prosperity.

Competition is our most valuable tool for promoting economic performance. No government and no bureaucratic planner can outperform the marketplace. Our free and admitted bias should be in favor of competition. We should wear the chip of competition on our shoulder, and we should dare the regulators to knock it off.

JUNE 30, 1977

It is the spur of competition that provides consumers with the better products and lower prices we seek. It is the preservation of competition that prevents a single firm or group of firms from controlling a market and substituting its judgment for that of the public. The private regulation of a market that results from control of pricing or other decisions by a single firm or group of firms is even more dangerous than control by government regulation.

APRIL 7, 1978

Although business leaders, government officials and academic economists continue to pay lip service to the conventional faith in free enterprise, that faith is often belied by what we are doing daily in reality. In case after case, both government and business are rejecting free-market solutions to public policy problems and resorting instead to government regulation. We are drifting from our moorings. The choice of competitive solutions to our economic problems is becoming a choice too little taken.

JUNE 30, 1977

The sad fact is that today small companies and private citizens are Davids without slingshots, competing against corporate and governmental Goliaths in wars of attrition which have become increasingly difficult to win.

The American people are not just concerned about "big government"; they are also concerned about the control exerted by "big business." The task of reducing concentrations of private economic power, and improving the capacity of individuals and small business to deal with the concentrations that remain, is just as important as the task of reducing the size of government.

AUGUST 7, 1978

111

There is an inconsistency between unaccountable corporate power and democratic values in this country. It is not just that government has grown too large and unresponsive, but that our economic institutions are out of scale and out of proportion.

Executives of the great corporations scoff at such feelings. They see them as nothing more than naïve nostalgia for a simpler life style no longer possible in today's complex modern world. But they are wrong. The need for scale and proportion in human institutions has always been recognized by thoughtful people. Aristotle had no difficulty understanding why democracy sprang from the small Greek city-state and not from the wealthy and powerful Persian Empire. The public is not clamoring for mom-and-pop stores served by horse-drawn delivery carts. What they fear is an unnecessary giantism in our institutions. The largest of our oil companies have already grown larger than many nations. Long ago they began to fit Edmund Burke's memorable description of the East India Company as "a state in the disguise of a merchant."

MAY 24, 1979

In many industries concentration is too high for effective competition, and this concentration is steadily increasing. Centralization of economic power has grown to the point where two hundred of our largest corporations control over two thirds of the domestic and foreign assets of all U.S. industrial corporations. The remaining 300,000 industrial corporations share what is left. The trend to ever increasing concentration is evidenced quite graphically by the fact that even after adjusting for inflation the top one hundred corporations controlled the same amount of assets in 1973 as the top two hundred corporations controlled in 1948.

The cost to the American consumer of this growing market power is unacceptable. Even the most conservative estimate of the inefficiencies and related costs of this market power has been placed at over $100 billion in 1977. This figure may in fact only scratch the surface of the true cost. For instance, many economists are now claiming that excessive market power has made impotent even the most basic tools for controlling inflation and unemployment.

FEBRUARY 28, 1978

There is something wrong with antitrust laws that give rise to perennial litigation against the same defendants. There is something wrong with antitrust laws that commit the government to litigation which spans decades. There is something wrong with antitrust laws that cannot deal with premeditated criminal conduct on the part of educated businessmen. There is something wrong with antitrust laws that cannot effectively restrain the concentrated activities of important industries in the United States today. And there is something wrong with antitrust laws that cannot stem mergers and acquisitions between corporate giants.

FEBRUARY 23, 1978

Consumer protection is not an abstract invention of the governmental bureaucracy, but a basic principle of the healthy marketplace.

OCTOBER 6, 1977

We had a taxpayers' revolution two hundred years ago, and we need another one today.

FEBRUARY 26, 1977

We have a tax crisis in America today because, for years, we have allowed taxes at all levels of government—federal, state, and local—to become vehicles of special privilege for the few, instead of the fair and reasonable income-raising measures they ought to be.

Tax reform can provide dollars to reduce the budget deficit; dollars for homes and jobs and schools and health; dollars for police and courts and drug control; dollars for the cities; dollars for capital formation; dollars for transportation and the environment; dollars to reduce the soaring burden of property and payroll taxes; dollars for revenue sharing with state and local governments—in short, dollars to meet all our urgent national priorities at home and around the world.

APRIL 13, 1976

If we are to bring relief to the hard-pressed taxpayers of this nation, let us do so in ways that do not destroy local tax systems that are the cornerstone of local control over local services in our federal nation, that do not turn tax relief for homeowners into tax windfalls for the property of big business.

If we are going to stop the hemorrhage of revenues wasted in massive spending designed to help the many who are poor, let us do so in ways that also stop the hemorrhage of revenues wasted in massive spending through tax loopholes designed to help the few who are rich.

If we are going to balance the federal budget, let us resolve that the burden will be shared by all—not just the cities, not just the poor and the black and the sick—so that no citizen pays too high a price for the cutbacks the future may have in store.

JUNE 19, 1978

People want an end to loopholes in the tax laws, so that those who eat at the most expensive restaurants will pay their way themselves, instead of making the Treasury foot the bill through tax deductions that are nothing more than food stamps for the rich.

SEPTEMBER 30, 1978

Few things are more calculated to destroy the confidence of ordinary taxpayers in the fairness of the nation's tax laws than the mushrooming suspicion that numerous provisions are being surreptitiously written into the laws for the special benefit of certain wealthy individuals and corporations. To some extent, it requires a Sherlock Holmes to detect a special-interest tax provision.

JUNE 28, 1976

The country can't afford large tax giveaways. The revenues to pay for them have to come from somewhere. That somewhere is usually the pockets of the 200 million average citizens, who have no loopholes because they have no lobbyists or lawyers putting the arm on Congress. They know that their taxes are too high because others pay too little.

AUGUST 2, 1976

The aim of tax reform is not to plow up the whole garden, but to get rid of the weeds so that we can let the flowers grow.

JULY 1, 1977

Today, the oil companies scored an impressive shale-oil victory in the Senate, overriding the interests of the state of Colorado.

The bus companies drove off with several hundred million dollars in Treasury prizes, apparently given out for the tax credit that produces the least energy saving.

The biggest winners of the day, however, were the eleven hundred largest corporations in America. In a clear Senate triumph over the average taxpayer, they have won $24 billion for converting from oil to coal.

If that report sounds fanciful to some, it is only because they have not read the bill before us. It is not difficult to identify the winners and the losers. The winners are the large corporations. They get the money. They pay less taxes. They continue to grow and expand their control over American business.

The losers are the average American taxpayers, whose hard-earned tax dollars are being used for these enormous tax subsidies.

OCTOBER 25, 1977

When it comes to spending federal dollars through the tax laws, the old labels do not fit the new realities. Typically, those in Congress who are the biggest budget cutters on direct federal subsidy programs also turn out to be the biggest spenders when it comes to subsidies through the tax laws. The biggest Scrooges are also the biggest Santas.

JANUARY 23, 1979

The argument for tax reform is much more than just an argument for equity among income groups, important as the goal of equity must be.

The effective operation of our tax system is also vital to our entire competitive free-enterprise system, and therefore to our democratic society itself.

Efficiency and equity: these are the twin goals of our tax system, and these are the goals that should guide us as we act on tax reform.

APRIL 13, 1976

A century ago, in concluding his address at the dedication of the battlefield at Gettysburg, Abraham Lincoln spoke of a new birth of freedom for the nation. There could be no finer judgment of the decade of the 1980s than for historians to say of these years that America met its economic challenge, that we achieved a new birth of competition for the nation, and that we restored our free enterprise system to its rightful place in our free society.

JUNE 14, 1979

PEACE AND STRENGTH

In foreign policy, we stand for peace with every nation, a defense strong enough to deal with any possible foe, and progress for the billions of people on this planet less fortunate than ourselves.

MAY 18, 1976

As we seek to improve the world in which we live and to secure its people against the scourge of war and want, we must understand that peace is not a final victory, but a continual effort.

DECEMBER 2, 1975

There is no priority for this nation higher than guaranteeing our national security and safety. Without an effective military force, and without a worldwide understanding that we have the unwavering will to use this force when our national interests are in danger, we unnecessarily place our way of life in peril.

JUNE 3, 1969

Our nation's finest historic role has been that of peacemaker—of helping to bring wars to a close and to create fresh conditions of security and prosperity in the world. In pursuing these tasks, we should recognize our own fundamental strengths. Despite the problems of energy and inflation, which we share with many other countries, the United States remains the world's strongest economy. Despite the challenges to free institutions everywhere, the United States remains a strong and resilient society which can meet any challenge facing us at home or overseas. Despite the military buildup of the Warsaw Pact and other countries, the United States has the most powerful military capability of any nation in the world, with strong and powerful allies in NATO, ANZUS and Japan.

FEBRUARY 20, 1979

The armed services continue to be a critical and worthwhile career for America's young men and women. If anything, it is now even more important for people of high caliber, committed to the nation's future, to serve in the armed forces.

New issues do not eclipse the old. Our future still depends on maintaining our military strength and preserving the nation from war. We must maintain the fully adequate strategic deterrent we have today.

FEBRUARY 17, 1975

We need a defense that is lean and powerful; with more muscle instead of fat; with a capacity to meet any threat to our security from Soviet military power or from any other source.

MARCH 17, 1976

In the swirl of immediate and pressing public issues, we sometimes tend to over-look the larger qualities that give meaning and hope to life—the eternal·shared values that are at the heart of civilization and give direction to the lives of our own citizens and to those of many different lands. Whatever the issues of the moment that may divide nations, we know that by increasing our understanding of one another, we lessen our conflicts and divisions.

OCTOBER 12, 1977

The central task which faces us is how to reconcile the support of detente with the advocacy of human rights. On the one hand, it is vital to nurture the relaxation of tension between East and West—the most fundamental human right remains freedom from war, which has twice swept the European continent in this century. On the other hand, it is the moral duty of statesmen not only to protect their citizens from violence within their societies, but to expand political, economic and social freedoms despite differences of ideology and social order.

JUNE 26, 1977

We are not the first great nation in history to find its ability to act reduced by changes taking place in the world. We are not the first to question its future role. But few great nations have had to adjust so quickly, and none has faced a world where there is no other nation or institution that can assume the major burdens that remain.

APRIL 11, 1975

During the late 1940s, when the continent of Europe faced uncertainty and even despair in the aftermath of war, people of vision in many lands joined together for the first time to rebuild economies that lay in ruin. Nations that had long stood aloof from one another in economic, political and even military struggle began to work together for the good of all. If Western leaders had that vision and commitment then, dare we have any less today?

NOVEMBER 15, 1974

In recent years, some Americans have become fearful of a new challenge from Europe. They see the European Community as potentially hostile to U.S. interests. I do not share that view. A strong, healthy, thriving Community is in the interest of nations on both sides of the Atlantic. It is also a precondition of future political and economic stability on the Continent.

DECEMBER 5, 1974

The 1980s should be a decade for Americans and Europeans of greater steadiness, mutual confidence and renewed commitment in our relations. It should be a decade of solid American support for the aspirations toward European unity reflected in the new, democratically elected European Parliament. It should also be a decade when Americans and Europeans work in even closer partnership in tackling our common global problems of peace and world security. Cooperation in the face of new challenges has been the essence of our transatlantic compact in the past and it will continue to be the essence of our alliance in the future.

MAY 7, 1979

I believe there are five basic challenges to the United States in today's world:

First, we continue to bear responsibility for preventing a nuclear war—mankind's final war. The need to end the nuclear arms race cannot wait.

Second, we must look to our traditional alliances and friendships abroad. The key to the way our allies see us lies in our conveying that we understand our own deeper national purpose; that we understand what is important to us in the world and what is not; and that we will place proper emphasis on relations with our closest friends abroad.

Third, we in the United States must remain concerned with helping to prevent conflict in other parts of the world. This means rededicating ourselves to helping bring the Arab–Israeli conflict to a close. We must lose no opportunity to help lift from the shoulders of Jew and Arab alike the terrible burden of conflict that has taken so many lives, blighted the hopes of millions of human beings, and set back the great promise of human development in that troubled part of the world.

Fourth, we can no longer be concerned only with these traditional areas of foreign policy. For in the world of economics—in the interdependence of nations —a wind of change is sweeping the world. From the mightiest industrial nation to

the poorest land on earth, basic economic changes are bringing a revolution to the global economy. We Americans are now finally and forever involved in the fortunes of other peoples. Isolationism may remain an illusion for some; it is a reality for none. We must increase our efforts to help lift from mankind the most enduring curse of the ages—the curse of poverty. We must respond, not because of the balance of power or even the global economy, but because it is right.

Finally, we in the United States must understand the importance of basic human rights in the conduct of our foreign policy. The world of relations among states is not really about power—as important as it is to meet the challenges that are posed by power. It is rather about the chance of each individual human being to build his own life and that of his family. It is about dignity. It is about hope. It is about a chance for human fulfillment through the qualities that God in His wisdom has given to humanity.

JUNE 14, 1976

The deepest threat to our real security today is our
failure to halt the race to Armageddon.

MAY 18, 1976

It does not take a million Hiroshimas to wreak untold destruction: it takes just one. One bomb in the hands of a nation or group disposed to use it would still raise unacceptable dangers. It would still threaten the lives of tens of thousands of people somewhere in the world.

APRIL 9, 1975

The city of Hiroshima stands as more than a monument to massive death and destruction. It stands as a living testament to the necessity for progress toward nuclear disarmament.

JANUARY 11, 1978

Never again should black rain fall.

JANUARY 30, 1978

The sand has been running through the hourglass
on many vital issues. Arms control is neglected,
while nuclear technology spreads and the world

feels less secure. Worldwide shortages of food and fuel and fertilizer threaten starvation and unrest for millions in other lands, but America too often stands aloof.

MAY 17, 1975

The overriding priority of the United States must be the prevention of nuclear war. Only by avoiding unparallelled destruction can we turn with confidence and hope to the great tasks of construction and social equity ahead of us.

FEBRUARY 24, 1978

There is no alternative to placing a brake on the nuclear arms race—no alternative unless we would accept the proliferation of nuclear weapons around the world; no alternative unless we are willing to accept an endless multiplication of weapons of massive destruction.

MARCH 7, 1977

We are told that the arms race must go on, because we may want to fight a "limited" nuclear war. Yet can anyone doubt that the number of people who would be killed in any nuclear war would be beyond our power to contemplate? Do we wish to make nuclear war more likely, by fostering the myth that only a few million deaths means a "limit"?

JUNE 24, 1975

We must all rededicate ourselves to forestalling the destructive application of nuclear energy—not merely for reasons of strategy, but for reasons of humanity. The nuclear arms race of the past generation is a tragic story of continuing folly in the face of the lessons of history.

JANUARY 11, 1978

By any measure, the United States is far and away the world's chief arms merchant.

DECEMBER 4, 1975

The sad reality is that the course, the pace and the objectives of arms control policies have been more influenced by the arms producers than by the arms controllers.

DECEMBER 2, 1975

We must stop accepting uncritically the notion that the sale of arms is an effective way to buy influence with foreign governments.

DECEMBER 4, 1975

We must hold the line against those who would make our common survival hostage to competition in other areas. How our two nations compete and cooperate is bound to affect the overall foreign and defense policies of the United States. But rejection of SALT will not increase Soviet respect for human rights or Soviet restraint in various parts of the world. Let the advocates of linkage explain how the cause of human rights in the Soviet Union will be served by a Senate refusal to ratify SALT. Let them explain how the stability of troubled regions will be enhanced by rejection of this treaty on the floor of the Senate. Let them explain how our security would be enhanced, and how the world would be a safer place, by failure to ratify SALT and by a return to Cold War confrontation.

FEBRUARY 20, 1979

If we approach SALT fairly on its merits, we will not accuse it of causing problems that predate it. We will not ask it to solve all of our defense problems. We will not rush into "solutions" for theoretical problems which will further diminish the security of both sides. And we will not hold SALT hostage to issues of less consequence to every American and Soviet man, woman and child. We are now at the threshold of a responsible SALT II agreement that will enhance our national security by preserving our military deterrent and by reducing the risk of a nuclear holocaust.

OCTOBER 8, 1978

A comprehensive test ban will make an important contribution to nuclear arms control. It will create a clear-cut barrier against all nuclear explosions, applicable to nuclear haves and nuclear have-nots alike; it will strengthen support for nonproliferation among the non-nuclear weapon states. It will significantly inhibit the development of new warheads and new weapons systems; it will help bring under control the increasingly troublesome qualitative aspects of the nuclear arms race.

FEBRUARY 24, 1978

While in the Soviet Union, I spoke of the strong commitment of the American government and the American people to human rights and social justice. I emphasized the depth of concern in the United States and other Western nations for Soviet dissidents, especially as symbolized by the trials of Anatoly Shcharansky and the other Soviet men and women of conscience sentenced over the past few months.

I also raised a large number of cases involving individuals wishing to emigrate. I am pleased to be able to report that the Soviet government has agreed to reconsider the cases of eighteen specific families. I have every expectation that all of these families will be permitted to leave for the United States or Israel in the very near future.

One of these cases involves Dr. Benjamin Levich, a world-renowned physical chemist and a member of the Soviet Academy of Sciences. Another involves Mr. and Mrs. Boris Katz and their daughter Jessica. The Katz family has attracted special concern in the United States because of Jessica's inability to digest normal food.

SEPTEMBER 11, 1978

This is an historic time for Asia. Three times in the past generation, Americans have sent their sons to fight and die in wars in Asia. Now for the first time since Pearl Harbor, we enjoy a sustained peace in that vital region. China and Japan now have friendly relations for the first time in this century. The United States now has friendly relations with both nations. We must build on these important and encouraging developments, in order to assure the future peace and prosperity of both Asia and the world.

JANUARY 17, 1978

Our close and enduring relationship with Japan is perhaps the best example in the world today of how two nations with different cultures in different parts of the world can find common bonds of friendship. The relationship is all the more unique because it has risen like a Phoenix from the ashes of a tragic war.

As a modern economic superpower, Japan should be in the vanguard among nations seeking to support the stability of the world economy. Together, we pride ourselves, and rightly so, on our capacity to find solutions to common problems and our ability to cooperate with other nations.

Through wise leadership and skillful statesmanship in both our nations, we have created a strong and enduring alliance between our two highly industrialized democracies. It is an alliance founded upon mutual benefit, mutual dependence, mutual trust, and mutual respect.

JANUARY 12, 1978

By some cruel paradox, an entire generation of young Americans and young Chinese have grown to maturity with their countries in a state of suspended war toward one another. Tragically, the world's oldest civilization and the world's most modern civilization, the world's most populous nation and the world's richest and most powerful nation, glare at each other across the abyss of nuclear war. We should proclaim our willingness to adopt a new policy toward China, a policy of peace, not war, a policy that abandons the old slogans, embraces today's reality, and encourages tomorrow's possibility.

MARCH 20, 1969

I believe we should now recognize Peking as the government of China. We should also withdraw our American military presence from Taiwan, while continuing to maintain intact our long-standing guarantees of the security of the island. Only by these sorts of important steps, I believe, can we convince Peking that we genuinely seek its full involvement in the world community.

FEBRUARY 5, 1971

Surely, in the entire history of American foreign policy there has never been a fiction more palpably absurd than the official American policy that the People's Republic of China does not exist, that the rulers of the fourteen million people on Taiwan are also the rulers of the hundreds of millions of Chinese on the millions of square miles of the mainland. It is as though the island of Cuba were to claim sovereignty over the whole continent of North America.

JUNE 24, 1971

There are some who say that the normalization of relations with Peking is a reflection of American weakness. I say the opposite. Normalization is a reflection of American strength—our strength to recognize the reality of nearly one billion people controlled not by Taipei but by Peking; our strength to act with responsibility to the seventeen million people on Taiwan, with whom we have enjoyed close ties for over three decades; our strength to consolidate and improve relations with the creative, industrious and rapidly modernizing Chinese people, and thus to contribute to the peace and stability not only of Asia but of the world.

FEBRUARY 14, 1979

The core of our approach to Taiwan should be the reconfirmation of our continuing interest in the peaceful resolution of the issue; provision for continuing defensive arms sales to Taiwan; consultation between the executive and legislative branches on any danger to the peace, prosperity, and welfare of Taiwan; and provision for meeting any such danger in accordance with our constitutional processes and legislative requirements, including the War Powers Act.

FEBRUARY 14, 1979

About nine-thirty in the morning, an hour out of Changsha, we drove past a large field, containing an army of ten thousand workers leveling a hill by hand to create more farmland. One by one in rows in single file, each worker, with a shoulder pole supporting two cane baskets, carried about forty pounds of dirt a trip from the top of the hill and dumped it at the bottom. Loudspeakers on poles at 100-yard intervals blared martial music, and a row of posts a quarter mile from the road provided a background propaganda quotation from Chairman Mao. A single small bulldozer smoothed the dirt that the workers dumped. Few moments so vividly captured the impression of a disciplined nation slowly on the move.

They will get their hills leveled and their factories modernized, but on a different time scale from the one we are accustomed to in the West. China is a year 2000 issue. It is a country intent on pulling itself up by its own bootstraps. In the past generation, the nation has moved from the Fourth World to the Third World, and they have their sights set on joining the Second World in my children's generation. By my grandchildren's generation, if the political center holds, they could be at

the top of the pole, among the superpowers they have so consistently shunned in the past.

The Chinese know they have time. They know they are far behind us, but they also know they are gaining. They will increasingly share in determining the balance between world war and world peace. The seeds we are planting and cultivating now will determine whether we will reap harmony or more hostility.

MARCH 1, 1978

In China, I was able to visit Johnny Foo and his family in Shanghai. Mr. Foo hopes to visit his mother and father in Stoneham, Massachusetts. I have just visited his parents' home in Stoneham this morning. I told them that the Chinese are now considering my request that their son be allowed to visit them.

JANUARY 17, 1978

In India I visited refugee areas along the entire border of East Bengal, from Calcutta and West Bengal in the west to the Jalpaiguri and Darjeeling districts in the north and to Agartala in the state of Tripura in the east. I listened to scores of refugees as they crowded into camps, struggling to survive in makeshift shelters in open fields or behind public buildings or trudging down the roads of West Bengal after days and even weeks of desperate flight. Their faces and their stories etch a saga of shame which should overwhelm the moral sensitivities of people throughout the world.

A fifty-five-year-old railway employee—he was a Muslim civil servant with thirty-five years of service—told me of an unexplained noontime attack by the Pakistani Army on his railroad station. "I do not know why they shot me," he said. "I don't belong to any political party. I was just a railway clerk." Now he sits idly in an Indian refugee camp, financially crippled, and with no prospect of returning to receive his long-earned government pension that was to begin next month.

AUGUST 26, 1971

136

I remember how Martin Luther King responded when he was criticized for protesting against the Vietnam War instead of confining himself to the area of civil rights. "I have fought segregation too long," he said, "for me to segregate my moral concerns."

APRIL 22, 1970

Vietnam is the most painful lesson we have ever learned about the aspirations of other peoples, and about events which are neither in our interest nor in our ability to control. Our involvement in the war was a mistake, a lengthy, costly, deadly, tragic mistake that blighted our own nation for more years than any other conflict since the Civil War. There was never a light at the end of the tunnel. There was only a long tunnel, made longer by our presence.

MAY 1, 1975

But the potential for escalation of the Indochina conflict remains. Over 100,000 Vietnamese forces are engaged in a protracted war in Cambodia, and over 50,000 Vietnamese forces occupy Laos. The Soviets have not only provided massive economic and military assistance to Vietnam, but have continued to provide logistic support for Vietnamese forces, and have deployed naval forces and used naval facilities both in Da Nang and in Cam Ranh Bay. A permanent Soviet military presence in Vietnam would have far-reaching political and military implications for the region, as well as for renewed great-power competition.

APRIL 2, 1979

Time and time again, it has been the people of Israel who have shown the courage, the genius and the determination to give substance to their dreams. Coming together from their roots in a dozen nations, they have vindicated the faith of their forebears. They are part of the Biblical prophecy, the prophecy that "I will bring them out from the peoples, and will gather them out of the countries, and will bring them to their own land."

JANUARY 13, 1975

138

In so many ways, the nations of America and Israel are alike. Both won bitter fights for independence. Both acknowledge the supremacy of moral law. Both believe in individual as well as national liberty. Both believe in democratic values and both are willing to sacrifice to achieve those values—values of justice, of peace and of equality.

OCTOBER 16, 1975

No American can travel an hour through the land of Israel without reacting from deep within to the stirring of ancient memories, the reawakening of one's own faith, the awareness that some long-proclaimed but long-delayed dream is unfolding before the eyes.

Despite the pain, despite the suffering, despite the personal anguish and even fear, the inheritance of Abraham is being reclaimed. There is a great sense of hope, an underlying confidence, a deep faith that there is new life surging up from the land itself, life that will not be denied.

MARCH 12, 1975

I have walked through the John F. Kennedy Memorial Peace Forest in Israel. Many of the five million young saplings have been planted with the help of Americans of all faiths. They reach deep into the soil of the Judean Hills now, and they stretch as far as the eye can see, across slopes that were barren less than a decade ago.

There is a sense that those roots bind this young and growing nation of Israel with its past—with the struggles, the sacrifices, and the martyrs of the Jewish people. They also bind together those who have never seen the nation of Israel, but who, by their gifts, have joined an epic struggle for renewal.

MAY 28, 1976

Events of the past weeks have dramatically reduced the atmosphere of distrust and misunderstanding between Egypt and Israel. Who would have predicted, even a month ago, that the President of Egypt and the Prime Minister of Israel would meet directly with each other in Jerusalem, to talk about a genuine peace? I for one believe that these two leaders have reached a profound, mutual commitment to serious negotiations, rather than resorting to the conflict which has repeatedly ravaged the Middle East.

NOVEMBER 29, 1977

The policy failure in Iran was massive, ranging from our intelligence to our commerce, diplomacy, and strategy. As a result, we lost major opportunities for modernization, moderation, and stability in the region. In vain, despite the lessons of

Vietnam, we poured virtually unlimited supplies of arms into Iran, in the hope that bombs and tanks and planes could somehow ensure the flow of oil to American homes and factories and lead to lasting peace in the Persian Gulf. Blinded by our growing dependence on the Shah for both energy and security, we ignored the repression and corruption of his regime, and we refused to recognize the signals of the growing storm.

We must move promptly now, not only to rebuild our essential relationship with Iran, but also to protect our other vital political, economic and security interests in the Middle East as a whole. With Egypt and Israel, we must move toward a comprehensive peace, not only in which their security is assured, but also in which their Arab neighbors begin to develop a shared interest in their common future. Here again, our Japanese and European allies can and should join in economic assistance to Egypt and other states which support the peace process, as part of an overall effort to develop incentives for peace and cooperation, instead of further polarization and conflict.

APRIL 2, 1979

Even without the bonds of blood and history, the deepening tragedy of Ulster today would demand that voices of concerned Americans everywhere be raised against the killing and the violence in Northern Ireland, just as we seek an end to brutality and repression everywhere.

OCTOBER 20, 1971

The Irish have loved their freedom in the past and they love their freedom now. They have fought oppression in all the ways in which history bears witness. Selfless and unselfish, Ireland has sent her sons and daughters, her physicians and priests, her songs and soldiers, her saints and scholars to countless other nations around the world. And everywhere they went, they took their cause of freedom with them.

The Irish yield to none in their role in the making of America. They have left their mark in every facet of American life. Wherever we look, in business and the labor movement, in literature and music and sports, in science and religion, in public service at every level of government, we find citizens of Irish descent who built our nation and helped to make it strong.

MAY 18, 1977

Consistently over the past eight years of violence in Northern Ireland, I have spoken out against the violence on both sides of this tragic conflict and against all forms of American support for the violence. I have also spoken out repeatedly against abuses of power by the security forces, both because of my abhorrence of

such law enforcement tactics in a democratic society and my firm belief that such tactics inevitably prove counterproductive. The moral authority of the police and the willingness of governments to admit and correct abuses are among the greatest hallmarks that distinguish free societies from totalitarian regimes.

JUNE 12, 1978

Whether American diplomats like it or not, real progress toward an honorable and just resolution of the Cyprus problem is crucial in repairing and revitalizing our traditionally good relations with the peoples and governments of both Turkey and Greece. And real progress on the Cyprus problem is also crucial in bolstering and stabilizing our security interests in the eastern Mediterranean. It is illusory to assume that these relations can be fully repaired and our interests fully stabilized without real progress on Cyprus.

APRIL 17, 1978

The first priority of the United States, in the eastern Mediterranean as well as elsewhere, must be to encourage a peaceful and just settlement of the conflicts that persist in Cyprus and the Aegean. It would be premature and dangerous for us to lift the arms embargo against Turkey until substantial progress is achieved. Our interests and assistance can be brought into balance, not by threats to end alliances, but by putting peace ahead of arms in this conflict-ridden part of the world.

APRIL 20, 1978

The tragic situation in Rhodesia is a cause of concern for all who care about the future of both whites and blacks in that country. It is of concern for all those who want peace in Africa. And it is a concern for all those who want to prevent a growth of Soviet and Cuban influence and activities in this part of Africa.

OCTOBER 14, 1978

The tragedy is that South Africa has lost in Steve Biko a moderate black figure of competence and intelligence. Instead of helping overcome the deep racial chasm in that tortured society—as he would have wished—he has become a symbol of hostility between the black majority and the white minority. And yet it was Steve Biko who wrote that he looked forward to a "non-racial, just and egalitarian society in which color, creed and race shall form no point of reference."

DECEMBER 6, 1977

In Africa, as in Asia and Latin America, we are being called upon to gain understanding, exercise good judgment, show compassion, and bring wisdom to our policies, where once we could get by with indifference and neglect.

The war in Angola is now over, and the wisdom of congressional action has been vindicated. We withdrew from a situation in which American arms would have intensified conflict and been paid for in African lives. We would have been remembered in Africa only for a tacit alliance with the forces of white racism and minority rule.

The time has long passed when we could afford to look at the nations and peoples of the African continent in terms of our relations with European countries —the former colonial powers. Today, policies based on the role of European nations in Africa are no longer relevant. The continent must be viewed for what it is: a set of individual nations and peoples, each with its own identity, its own aspirations, its own problems and promise.

We face a critical choice that can no longer be put off. Will America support peoples of Africa who seek only the "unalienable rights" we sought and won ourselves two centuries ago? Or will we continue to follow policies that isolate us from these peoples—policies that place us on the side of minority governments that deny basic human rights, and that invite the involvement of other outside powers?

MARCH 23, 1976

If there is a single element in our posture toward Latin America that symbolizes an archaic Cold War strategy, it is the effort to isolate the Republic of Cuba.

The isolation of Cuba today stems from events which occurred at the start of

142

the decade, but the history of our relations spans the entire life of that nation. However clumsy our efforts in the Spanish-American War, the end result was an independent Cuba. But from that time forward, we acted toward the Pearl of the Antilles with overbearing protectiveness.

OCTOBER 12, 1971

The Panama Canal treaties are in our best political interests, for they recognize Panama as an equal partner, not a colony, in assuring a safe, secure, and open canal. All of Latin America, and indeed the world, is watching as we decide whether to cling to the last vestiges of colonialism or to establish new, mature, equal relationships with the weak as well as the strong.

MARCH 3, 1979

What we need is more facts and fewer public-relations efforts about the tragic problems besetting Argentina. The human rights situation in that country is today as serious as ever. Amnesty International estimates that some fifteen thousand Argentine men, women, and children have simply disappeared since the 1976 military coup; in addition, as many as ten thousand have been officially detained.

143

Argentina's government lists include the names of only 3,500, although thousands more are known to be in prison. In the past one hundred days alone, Amnesty International has received reports of over one hundred disappearances, and there are fears that many more have disappeared as well. Thousands of the detainees have been murdered and nearly all political prisoners have been tortured by the security forces. This torture and killing continue to the present time.

OCTOBER 14, 1978

We have come a long way since the Congress terminated military assistance to Chile in 1976—against the wishes of an Administration that found it impolitic to oppose the Pinochet junta which it had helped to bring to power. But to finally achieve the results we desire, the United States government must press persistently and consistently for human rights and democracy in Chile. It must be heard not only by the generals of Santiago, but by the Chilean people and the American people as well.

JULY 24, 1978

The United States has a special historic responsibility to the people of Nicaragua. It was the United States Marines who established and trained what the State Department has referred to as "the personal instrument" of the Somoza family for forty years—the Nicaraguan National Guard and its auxiliary paramilitary formations. It has been the United States Agency for International Development that has provided the Somoza regime with almost fifteen percent of its annual governmental expenditures. It has been U.S. security assistance that has both trained and maintained the present National Guard and its paramilitary auxiliaries. And it is our continuing military aid in particular that indicates to the Somoza regime and the world that we continue to condone prevailing conditions of arbitrary arrest, political suppression, murder and atrocity.

AUGUST 4, 1977

The American people do not accept a chessboard view of the world, based only on power politics. Our policy must have a surer foundation, grounded in our basic humanitarian values as a nation.

MAY 27, 1976

What we do in the outside world must be based on a deep moral sense of our purpose as a nation. Without that sense of our enduring heritage—the values on which this nation was founded, the basic compassion and human concerns of our people—there is little we can do both for ourselves and for others. American involvement in the outside world must reflect what is best in our heritage, and what is best in ourselves. Our moral commitment to peoples of the world is not to an army, not to this regime or that government, not to this official or that political faction. Our true obligations are with people and with the issues and problems that affect all humanity.

JUNE 14, 1976

We must recommit ourselves to a spirit of cooperation with other nations, both rich and poor. We learned a generation ago that two broad oceans offer no real military security. Now we are learning that our economy is also not isolated from the harsh winds of change that are sweeping the world. American jobs, American prices, and American incomes are vitally affected by what happens abroad.

FEBRUARY 17, 1975

Building a new framework of cooperation between the developed world and the developing world has become one of the major challenges of the final quarter of this century. We have an opportunity to move away from military confrontation to economic cooperation, from the pursuit of militant and narrow national interests to the pursuit of broader international development.

JANUARY 12, 1978

The growing interdependence among nations of the globe is a phenomenon as striking today as the interdependence of the tiny colonies that came together on our shores two hundred years ago.

MAY 27, 1977

The waters of the seas that wash upon the shores of Asia are the same waters that wash upon the shores of the United States. The currents of the oceans that sweep majestically along the coasts of the United States are the same currents that sweep along the coasts of Africa and India and Latin America.

JANUARY 12, 1978

We cannot ignore the fact that the poorer two thirds of the world's population continues to live at or below the level of minimum subsistence, while less than one third of the world's population consumes eighty-five percent of the world's production. We cannot ignore their faces pressed against our windows. We cannot ignore their silent cries for help.

JANUARY 12, 1978

Four years ago, a few days before the Saigon government collapsed, the Chu family made a desperate flight from Vietnam, arriving in the United States with a few suitcases of clothes and family mementos. But last Sunday, at the graduation ceremonies at Catholic University, the four Chu children all graduated together, and with the highest academic honors. The story of the Chu family continues one of the oldest themes in our nation's history. Refugees coming to our shores never really burden our resources. They enrich our society and culture and contribute to our nation's strength and well-being.

MAY 15, 1979

In Southeast Asia, the plight of homeless people has reached crisis proportions. In recent days we have faced a repetition of some of the worst and most tragic events of the 1930s—of desperate, homeless refugees being carted off to their deaths—of refugee boats being shoved out to sea—of countless thousands languishing in camps, uncertain each day about what the future may bring. Every day for the past twelve months, the crisis has grown steadily worse—overwhelming the ability of the international community or local governments to cope.

JUNE 18. 1979

America will always have an open door for refugees from other lands. To the dispossessed and homeless of the world, the Statue of Liberty means more than just a symbol of a new life. It may mean life itself.

MARCH 4, 1979

The American people have responded generously and compassionately to the needs of homeless people. A national policy of welcome serves our country and traditions well. We must help ensure greater equity in our treatment of refugees and displaced persons and establish a more orderly procedure for their admission into the United States in reasonable numbers.

MARCH 15, 1978

As citizens of the world's oldest republic, whose sons "fired the shot heard round the world," we cannot be deaf to the voices of other people straining to be heard, of people struggling to share in freedom. And once we learn this lesson, America will again be a symbol of hope and freedom for people in other lands.

MAY 1, 1975

THE PROMISE
OF AMERICA

Like my brothers before me, I pick up a fallen standard. Sustained by the memory of our priceless years together, I shall try to carry forward that special commitment to justice, to excellence, and to courage that distinguished their lives.

AUGUST 21, 1968

The age-old virtues that built this country and made it great are the same virtues that will keep us strong today. Faith and sacrifice, work and duty, truth and justice, respect for the rights of others—so long as we hold these values dear and strive to instill them in our children, the spirit of America will be rekindled anew in each succeeding generation.

MAY 26, 1976

Our problems today call less for ringing repetitions of old battle cries than for a boldness of thought and action that matches the boldness of our history. It is a time when we cannot afford polite evasions. Rather, we must speak with the candid and sometimes painful honesty that is the mark of one's deepest friends.

MAY 7, 1978

We have great dreams, and we have a great opportunity to make those dreams come true.

FEBRUARY 28, 1976

We do not need more study. We do not need more analysis. We do not need more rhetoric. What we need is more leadership and more commitment.

JULY 27, 1972

I refuse to believe that America is ungovernable, or that the problems on the nation's plate today are more difficult than the ones we faced in other critical periods of our history.

To name them is to refute the analogy. The achievement of independence, the emergence of the Constitution from the failures of the Articles of Confederation, the spanning of a continent, the preservation of the Union in the face of civil war, the transformation to a powerful industrial economy, the recovery from the Great Depression, the victory in World War II and the rebuilding of Europe and Japan, the revolution in civil rights—surely, the crises we face today are no greater in magnitude than these challenges of the past.

APRIL 30, 1979

Let us seek the courage, the wisdom, the faith, and the compassion to do what is right in the years to come. Let us be proud of our communities and our country. Let us be proud of our great traditions, confident that our brightest days still lie ahead, hopeful that we too can share in the betterment of our society in the time that is given us on earth.

MAY 27, 1977

It is from the family that we gain the strength, the hope, the aspirations, the guidance, and the support to be effective and productive members of society. It is from the family that we learn to produce wholesome and viable communities where individual talent and creative initiative can enjoy the fullest expression.

SEPTEMBER 11, 1976

The strength of the family is our greatest national treasure. It was the bond that helped the first settlers endure the incredible physical hardships of this land at the beginning of our nation. It has been the cornerstone of our national growth and strength throughout the two hundred years of our history. And it is still the central influence that will determine the path of our nation's future in the years to come.

MAY 26, 1976

In a sense, our task is like that of Michelangelo, who saw his masterpieces as prisoners released from enormous blocks of marble. We need the same sort of attitude and skills and vision now. We need to free the people of this country to do all the jobs they can do so well. We need to make our great system of free enterprise and competition work.

OCTOBER 18, 1978

Traveling across the length and breadth of America, taking the measure of our people, you cannot help but come away with a sense that we can do the job—that our problems are only human, and the solutions will be human, too; that America is a land whose people have the capacity to solve its problems many times over, if only we let them try.

JUNE 15, 1971

There has been a growing sense among all of us over the past decade—a growing sense that no matter what each and every one of us as individuals wants or does, there is no one to listen and respond. Decisions are made over which we have no control; actions are taken with which we may disagree, but there is no way to let that disagreement be known. The city, the state, the national government just seem to keep working away, almost as if they had a life of their own—no longer responding to the complaint about the way in which we live in crowded cities with noise and dirt and countless impersonal injustices, no longer responding to the people. In the past decade, it seems as if we have become more and more like a machine that stamps us out to work in the morning, cranks us through the day, and drops us off at night.

But this is not what America is supposed to be. This is not why, two hundred years ago, brave men stood in Charlestown on Bunker Hill and took the charge of the English.

It was for different things. We dreamed then and we dream now of a nation that respects the individual dignity of every man. Then as now people wanted their talents and worth recognized so that their lives would be meaningful, not spent in daily conflicts with each other. Then as now our hope was for a nation that would be tolerant. The United States didn't grow for two hundred years to arrive in an atmosphere of turmoil and self-doubt. Somewhere, somehow, we have lost our way. Somewhere, somehow in the past decade we lost sight of our own greatness and the promises that the American revolution made to the world.

JUNE 17, 1970

Our own experience has been tempered by tragedy, by the burdens of responsibility, by a foreign policy that has too often been cut loose from its deep moral roots. Yet in that experience of two centuries the seeds of common cause with the rest of mankind remain. We are not a people too paralyzed to act in the outside world, too preoccupied with our own problems, too calloused by the past. Rather we are a people whose time of inspiration, of leadership, is still unfolding; a nation of basic strengths requiring only a renewed sense of moral purpose to lead us to new greatness in the future.

APRIL 12, 1976

154

The new decade will be an unusual one, because of the juxtaposition of two symbolic years—1984, with its Orwellian connotations, and 1987, the two-hundredth anniversary of the American Constitution.

What goals shall we set for the nation in the decade of the nineteen eighties? What trails shall we try to blaze, whose compass shall we use to find direction? How shall we—how shall our children and our grandchildren—remember it?

Will it be a rising sun or a setting sun, a forward step in the journey toward fulfillment of the American dream, or a backward step in the nostalgic search for a simpler past that can never be recaptured?

Will it be a time of new action and inspiration, as when America moved from the decade of the fifties to the sixties? Or will it be a time of continuing reaction, of drift among the surging tides of events beyond our ability to control?

Will it be a time of constructive reappraisal of our government and its relations with the people, worthy of the bicentennial of our unique and living Constitution? Or will it be just another raucous holiday with fireworks and costumed reenact-ments—fitting perhaps for the 1976 bicentennial of independence, but hardly appropriate for commemoration of the events of 1787?

Let us resolve that private interest shall not prevail over the public good. Let us pledge that when our children and grandchildren look back on this new decade, they will remember it as another of those great historic eras in which America flowered, in which the nation's spirit and vitality rose to meet the challenge—a decade, in short, in which the promise of America once again was met.

APRIL 30, 1979

Often, all it takes to turn the tide is one individual, acting alone and against the odds. A single voice of courage and understanding can change the flow of events and improve the community in which we live. Sometimes, it can alter the course of history.

JUNE 11, 1976

Let us give something back to America, in return for all it has given us.

MARCH 1, 1976

158

PHOTO CREDITS